Work Worldwide

International Career Strategies
for the Adventurous Job Seeker

by Nancy Mueller

John Muir Publications
A Division of Avalon Travel Publishing

John Muir Publications
A Division of Avalon Travel Publishing
5855 Beaudry Street
Emeryville, California 94608

Printed in the United States of America
First edition. First printing March 2000

Library of Congress Cataloging-in-Publication data

Mueller, Nancy, 1950-
    Work worldwide : international career strategies for the adventurous job seeker /
by Nancy Mueller
    p. cm.
    ISBN 1-56261-490-8
    1. Employment in foreign countries. 2. Job hunting. 3. Vocational guidance.
4. Americans—Employment—Foreign countries. I. Title.

HF5382.55   M83 2000
650.14—dc21   99-057943

Editors: Peg Goldstein, Bonnie Norris
Production: Kathleen Sparkes, Janine Lehmann
Interior Design: Kathleen Sparkes, Janine Lehmann
Cover Design: Janine Lehmann
Cover Illustration: William Rotsaert
Typesetting: Kathleen Sparkes
Printer: Publishers Press

Distributed to the book trade by
Publishers Group West
Berkeley, California

Dedication

To my husband, John, with great love and gratitude, for your care and feeding of my soul as an artist

Acknowledgments

Many thanks go to many people for helping me see this book through to completion. I am particularly grateful to my mother for planting the seeds of adventure and writing that have blossomed into this book and to my workshop participants for sharing their triumphs and frustrations in finding work internationally.

I'd also like to thank Dr. Henriette Anne Klauser for showing me how to write down my dream of publishing this book and how make it happen; Dr. Sondra Thiederman, role model, coach, and mentor; Carol Keefe and Robin Ryan for their encouragement in the early days of this project; Tom Bell, fellow writer, motivator, and steadfast supporter; Linda Thompson at the Boeing Corporation; Linda and Dan Stokes at Prism International, Inc.; expatriates Marshall Whitehead II, Jack Landstrom, Cherie Ohlson, Mike Devoll, Harriet Selkowitz, Jerry Galloway, Anne Adolphson, Bill Fontana, Gail Hayes, Craig Ventimiglia, Debra Eller, Gail Howerton, Richard Andresen, Barry Scammell, Bonnie and Ken Peterson, and Kris and Rick Beckwith; NSA colleagues Mary Kay Kurzweg, Kathie Hightower, Winston Hall, Carla Cross, and Steve Miller; friends Les and Shigeko Podgorny, Helene Greissler, Karen Unger Sparks, Kim Frerichs, Miguel Valenciano, and Roger and Candy Kovner Bel Air; and reference librarians at the Seattle Public Library and Bellevue City Library. Special thanks go to the staff at John Muir Publications for their help in getting *Work Worldwide* to press and marketplace.

Contents

Foreword

It takes an adventurous spirit to work internationally. It also takes courage, intelligence, and a thorough knowledge of how to work effectively with people and systems that are usually unfamiliar and always complex.

The adventurous, courageous, and intelligent among you may feel equipped and ready to go. Well, the bad news is, it takes more than the right personality and latest jet-lag remedy to create, keep, and enjoy an international career. It takes knowledge—such as knowing that boasting is a surefire way not to get a job in Asia, that a handwritten cover letter is often more impressive to an employer in Europe than that perfectly typed opus, and that the culture shock encountered by expatriates when coming home is often far more painful than even the most befuddled moment overseas.

The good news is that *Work Worldwide* is here to help. Nancy Mueller and the expatriates she interviewed for this book have lived it. They have made mistakes, scored the successes, and learned the lessons of working overseas. Maybe these lessons can't immunize you against every embarrassing international faux pas, but they will go a long way toward helping you obtain the international career of your dreams.

—Sondra Thiederman, Ph.D.
Cross-Cultural Communications

Introduction

When you imagine working abroad, what do you think of? What pictures come to mind? If you're like many people, your answers might include words like "adventure," "romance," "excitement," "variety," "exotic ports of call," "fame and fortune," "foreign languages," and "cultures."

Maybe you're looking for a lifestyle in which you can grab a warm baguette on your way home from work in Paris. Perhaps your ideal lunch break at the office is a mackerel sandwich washed down with a beer in Amsterdam. Maybe you dream of waking up to the sound of the muezzin calling the faithful to prayer in Cairo or see yourself catching some sun on Ipanema Beach after a rewarding day of work in Rio de Janeiro. Perhaps you imagine the haze of urban Tokyo parting long enough for you to glimpse Mount Fuji rising in the distance from your office window. You might even picture living a lifestyle similar to Indiana Jones or James Bond. And why not? Overseas employment can mean some or all of these scenarios—but that's only part of the picture.

Working abroad also means taking care of peripheral issues that will affect your ability to be successful in your job. You'll need to find a place to live, learn about banking and shopping, and find out how best to get around while based in another country. You might have to balance your work life with a newly transplanted family or personal life. You might have periodic feelings of confusion and frustration—you might not understand what someone is saying to you, or you might get lost because you can't read road signs.

I was once late to a business appointment in Milan because, even though I knew where I needed to go, the cab driver refused to take me there. I could understand that much—but not his reason, since I don't speak Italian. Thirty minutes later, after attempting to communicate with half a dozen cab drivers and more than a few well-meaning bystanders, I finally understood that the street I needed to reach was closed to traffic. Eventually, the driver got me within walking distance, and I arrived at my appointment—luggage in tow—an hour late. I was met by my four Italian hosts who remained unsmiling, with arms folded, during my entire sales presentation.

I don't want this type of problem to happen to you, but if it does, I want you to be prepared. I want you to reach for the sky as you explore the international job market, but I also want you to keep your feet firmly grounded in reality—with your eyes wide open at the same time.

WHY GO GLOBAL?

As you consider working abroad, you may have some lingering doubts about how it will benefit you in the long run. Let's look at what you can hope to get out of going global. First of all, you can expand your sources of revenue—that is, make money! Discovering how to do business across cultures isn't easy and it doesn't happen overnight, but the payoffs can be rich. A 1996 report on global relocation trends stated that 43 percent of revenues are generated outside of countries in which businesses are headquartered. And it's not only Fortune 500 companies, such as Boeing and Federal Express, that are going global. Smaller manufacturing and high-tech companies are also doing business overseas. For example, Lynn and Nathan, a Seattle-based couple and proprietors of a high-tech sonar equipment manufacturing company, began exporting in their second year of business. Currently, they estimate that more than 40 percent of their revenue is generated outside of the United States. If you own a small business, you too might consider growing your business abroad to expand your profits.

When you work abroad you also have the potential for personal and professional growth—there is nothing quite like moving abroad to gain an entirely new perspective on your life. As writer and diplomat James Russell Lowell said, "Wise men travel to discover themselves." Your learning curve will increase quickly when familiar ways of doing business no longer work, and you are forced to "think outside the box." In the process, you can uncover new opportunities for using your talents and expertise, while gaining additional knowledge, skills, and experience in an international environment. This hard-won overseas experience can improve your marketability and translate into increased pay, job promotions, and better benefit packages—whether you continue to work abroad or decide to return to the United States. Demonstrating your ability to work within different cultures and to master unexpected challenges increases your competitiveness in our rapidly expanding global marketplace. Discovering how to cope, adapt, and succeed abroad will raise your self-confidence and enable you to better meet other difficult situations that life may throw your way in the future.

An additional benefit of working abroad is the vast international network that you can tap into—not only for future job opportunities around the world but also for personal fulfillment. In short, answering the call to work abroad is synonymous with answering the call to have an adventure—and perhaps fulfill a lifelong dream and change your life.

WHO WORKS ABROAD?

Who works abroad? People just like you. Working expatriates are many and varied, including seasoned executives who are hired for the short- or long-term to fill strategic management positions. These may be new jobs, created to establish a base of operations in a particular country, or already established positions. Expatriates also include globetrotters who have made a career of pursuing job opportunities around the world, professionals who reside in the United States but do frequent business abroad, employees who are working abroad to develop their knowledge and skills used at home, partners of professionals sent abroad, and adventurers seeking income to finance their travels around the world or retirement overseas. Here are some examples:

Andy is an international sales manager for a marine and fisheries company in Seattle. He travels to Asia two or three times a year for a couple of weeks at a time. Since Andy is also busy raising two preschoolers, this position satisfies his desire to spend time at home yet still work internationally.

Jaime opened her own Japan–United States business communications and relations company "out of sheer frustration," when she was unable to find a position in the United States after spending two years in Japan. Though based in the United States, she travels to Asia frequently.

Marie is a certified translator and simultaneous interpreter. She translates technical documents from English into French and travels around the world as an interpreter at international conferences.

When a longtime business associate asked Michael if he knew anyone who might be interested in an international assignment, Michael asked to be considered. Nine months later, he was on his way to a two-year assignment with an international wireless group in Hong Kong.

HOW DID THEY DO IT?

Andy, Jaime, Marie, and Michael each succeeded in finding work in the international marketplace. Despite the differences in their backgrounds, foreign assignments, and motivations for working overseas, the four share important characteristics. They all started with a clear picture of what kind of work they wanted. They also stayed the course in their quest to find an international position, even though they faced obstacles along the way. They discovered how to make their dreams a reality, and, in the end, found work abroad. Andy, Jaime, Marie, and Michael also prove, however, that there is no one "right way" to get an international job.

CAN I FIND WORK ABROAD, TOO?

Yes, you *can* have an international job—if you know what work you want and where you want to live, and if you're willing to do your homework. Perhaps you are just starting to think about working abroad, or you have done some preliminary research but have reached a fork in the road. You are wondering if it's a detour or a dead-end. Perhaps you are bogged down with information and are feeling frustrated trying to sort through all of it. Maybe you are not sure which questions to ask.

Some of you are looking for alternatives to the traditional nine-to-five job. Others are looking for adventure or the sense that your work makes a difference. Maybe you've been laid off from your job temporarily or permanently and hadn't considered going international until you picked up this book. Perhaps you want to be based in the United States, with only occasional travel overseas.

Whatever your aspirations or position—seasoned professional, world traveler, or college student—this book will help you pinpoint the information you need so that you can succeed in getting international employment. It is a resource that you can pick up and use immediately, regardless of where you are in your quest. Return to the book time and time again as your goals, experiences, and interests change.

I want you to get started, persevere, and succeed in getting international employment. I wrote this book to help you do just that—as quickly and easily as possible. The book highlights essential strategies for getting work abroad and specific steps to help you succeed. Yet only you can choose the path that suits your skills and desired lifestyle. That's what makes this kind of search both exciting and challenging. As you begin your personal odyssey, you may discover things about yourself that will surprise and delight you. Undoubtedly, you will make some new friends along the way. One thing is certain: Once you begin to explore the possibilities and opportunities within international employment, your life will never be the same again.

Here are a few important guidelines to keep in mind as you begin your global job search. First, there are no rules about how to secure international employment. If you're looking for the "right way" to go about your job search, the bad news is there isn't one. The good news is that there are *unlimited* ways to find the international job that's right for you. This book will give you valuable tips to save you time, money, and heartache in the process.

Remember also that an international job is usually not a unique position in itself, but rather is a counterpart to a position you might find in the United States. The work might be the same. What's different is where the work is done and, often, how it's done. The success stories woven throughout this book have one thing in common: Each person who found work abroad built upon his or her previous experience to chart a new path overseas.

Finally, remember that getting an international position requires determination, a belief in your ability to succeed, discipline, and perseverance. It also involves a lot of hard work and relationship building. Expect to spend time doing homework and expect some frustration. Those who *don't* succeed in finding work abroad often have unrealistic expectations of how long the search will take, what help they can expect from others along the way, and how far their credentials and previous experience can take them. When those expectations aren't met, they give up on their global job search. Don't you give up on your dream of working abroad. Sure, you will have to do a lot of work, but this book will show you how to succeed.

Now it's your turn. Use this book as a guide, and consider me your personal coach as you begin your international job odyssey. The book was not written with the intent that you would sit down and read it from beginning to end, but rather that you would use it in a way that suits your specific career needs. I encourage you to do the exercises that will help you achieve clarity, reach your goals in the shortest time possible, and have fun along the way. Use the information presented here—and your own imagination—as a springboard to international employment success.

1

Get Started—Focus!

Afoot and light-hearted I take to the open road,
Healthy, free, the world before me,
The long brown path before me leading wherever I choose.
—*Walt Whitman*

"My school friends . . . agreed that cutting open mummies and searching gold-filled tombs were perfectly rational goals and were well worth pursuing," explains Egyptologist Kent R. Weeks, discussing his career dreams. Perhaps such goals seem farfetched, but Weeks put his vision into action and went on to discover the lost tomb KV5.

Do you have a vision about working abroad? Try to put it into words—either to yourself or, better yet, to someone who cares about you and can give you objective feedback. Give your description in 30 seconds or less. Remember to be specific. Go ahead. I'll wait.

How did it go? Were you able to state precisely what type of work you want, where you want to work, and for whom? If so, go to the head of the class! If, on the other hand, you had difficulty articulating what type of work you want, where you want to work, and for whom, not to worry. You're still on the right track. You just need a little help in bringing your goals into clearer focus. As German poet Johann Wolfgang von Goethe wrote, "Whatever you can do, or dream you can, begin it."

In this chapter, you will discover the essential attributes for overseas success. You will have the opportunity to figure out exactly what type of international job you want, where you want to live and work overseas, and how to create realistic plans and time lines for achieving your global goals.

You will find key information that will help you evaluate your background, skills, credentials, and experience.

W HERE IN THE WORLD DO YOU WANT TO LIVE?

Have you ever looked at a world map and thought about where you'd live if you could go anywhere? Most of us have done so at one time or another. Spend some time right now thinking about where you might like to go.

Of course, if you're truly adventurous and you don't know where you want to work abroad—and don't particularly care as long as it's overseas—you could always pin a map on a dartboard, hang it on your wall, throw a dart, and go wherever your dart lands. Or you could close your eyes, spin a globe, point to a place, open your eyes, and see where you end up. Based on how you feel when you see what part of the world you've blindly selected, you can begin to zero in on where you do and don't want to work overseas. There are, however, other ways to discover what kind of work you want to do and where you want to live abroad.

D EFINE YOUR GLOBAL VISION

"I'm a business executive who travels overseas occasionally for my company. I'd eventually like to start my own global consulting firm."

Great. You're already traveling abroad on business with your employer picking up the tab. Now is the time to develop your base of international contacts for future reference. I'm not talking about taking away your employer's business or doing anything unethical, but I am suggesting that you take advantage of your time abroad to do some research. Can you tack a few extra vacation days onto your trip to find and follow up on business leads? Do as much research as possible before your trip and set up appointments before you go.

Once you're overseas, take advantage of conferences you might be attending to actively network and research companies and organizations. Check out job advertisements in the local newspaper. Stop by the

American Chamber of Commerce to look at their resources and offer to give a presentation to market your services.

"I'm still in school, but I know I want to live and work abroad as soon as I can after graduating."

Wonderful. Several steps you can take now will set the foundation for a long- or short-term adventure overseas. Use the time and resources you have in school to research internships that can take you overseas while you're still a student. That way, you can get a feel not only for a future career but also for what it's like to live and work in another country.

Add classes in international business or trade, foreign languages, and cross-cultural know-how to your curriculum. Join campus associations that have a global focus. Travel abroad on your summer vacations. All of these efforts can increase your desirability to an international recruiter or employer.

Travel enthusiast Rick Steves began his annual trips to Europe while still a student. To pay the cost of his airline tickets, he borrowed from his parents, gave piano lessons, and later became a tour guide. Rick soon developed a niche in teaching people about independent travel skills. He's parlayed his love affair with Europe into a thriving business enterprise, complete with tour packages, travel guidebooks, and a popular video series.

"I'm retired. I've been thinking about going to live abroad for a time—maybe even permanently, if I like it. I'd like to earn some extra income by working part-time overseas."

Sounds good. One thing you might want to consider first is checking out international consulting opportunities with your former employer. Today, more companies than ever before are setting up branch operations overseas, where they can be more visible and responsive to their global customer needs. Temporary contractors work on assignments from three to six months on average and are cheaper and easier for organizations to manage. If you're interested in longer term job assignments, try connecting with a U.S. company that has branch offices where you'd like to live.

Ken took a different approach. After he retired from his job at the Boeing Corporation, he and his wife, Bonnie, went to China to teach English for a year. They hooked up with a credible agency that made the arrangements and supported them throughout their stay abroad.

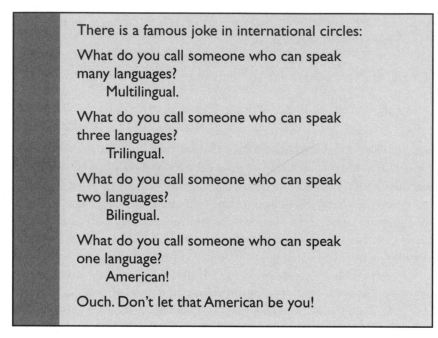

There is a famous joke in international circles:

What do you call someone who can speak many languages?
  Multilingual.

What do you call someone who can speak three languages?
  Trilingual.

What do you call someone who can speak two languages?
  Bilingual.

What do you call someone who can speak one language?
  American!

Ouch. Don't let that American be you!

"I have no idea what I want to do. I just know that I'm burned out in my current job, and I'm looking for more adventure in my life."

As Yogi Berra said: "You got to be very careful if you don't know where you're going, because you might not get there." Your goal of working abroad needs to be specific. Let's face it: it's hard to hit a moving target. You need to determine what kind of work you want to do overseas, what type of organization you want to work for, where you want to live, when you want to go and for how long, and why you want to go. You might have a vague sense of restlessness and a longing to go overseas, but you'll need a stronger focus than that to realize your dream of living and working abroad.

Yes, you can still find a job overseas even if you don't know what kind of work you want, but your search will probably take longer. And you may end up accepting *any* employment offer as long as it gets you overseas— only to discover that you dislike the job. Then what? And add this frustration to the cultural adjustments you'll be going through in a foreign country. For these reasons, you'll be much better off doing a bit of homework up front to prevent a calamity halfway around the world.

HOW, WHAT, AND WHERE?

When considering your significant job skills, keep in mind what many career specialists refer to as your "motivated" job skills. In other words, think about not only what strengths you possess but also, perhaps more importantly, what you consistently enjoy doing and do well. You may be a gifted artist, for example, but unless you're inspired to use that skill professionally and not just as a hobby, you'll lack the motivation to perform at your best.

To determine how your perception of your skills compares with that of others, look for patterns among the performance reviews or letters of recommendation you have received. Is there a match between what others highlight as your effective skills and accomplishments and how you see yourself? To do a more detailed analysis of your job skills, you'll find a number of effective resources at the end of this chapter.

If you don't know what type of work you want to do overseas, you can't know whether or not you have the necessary background and experience to perform the job successfully. If you do know the kind of international work you want, then you can research the type of skills you'll need and determine whether you'll need additional training—academic or otherwise—to meet your job goals abroad.

Focus also means being clear about where you want to live abroad. You can better direct your job efforts if you know that you want to live in Spain, for example, as opposed to Sri Lanka. Focus is good, but flexibility is still important, in the event that you are unable to locate the job you want in Spain. It may be enough, as a starting point, to know that you want to live in Europe first of all, then Germany, then Munich in particular if given the opportunity. Or, you might want to live where you can speak Spanish. If you can't find a job in Venezuela, maybe another Spanish-speaking country in Latin America will do just fine.

It also helps to know what type of organization you want to work for, so you can concentrate solely on those organizations that meet your criteria. Then you can dig a little deeper to assess whether a particular organization matches your philosophy and values. The better the fit, the easier time you will have adjusting to living and working abroad. You will want to be certain you understand the company's job requirements, salary offer, and benefits package. The more you know about the organization and what you can expect up front, the fewer problems you'll encounter overseas. You may discover things about a company that make it less than an ideal match for you—yet still decide to accept a job offer. At least you will have done so with your eyes wide open. When you know the type of work you want to do, where you want to do it, and for whom, you're that much closer to finding the right international position.

WHAT DOES IT TAKE TO SUCCEED ABROAD?

In a 1995 survey among members of the National Foreign Trade Council (NFTC), 96 percent of respondents reported that personality traits and interpersonal style were the major factors contributing to failed international assignments. Incredible, isn't it? What this means to you is that you might very well receive an international job offer based on your technical competence. Yet, unless you can adjust to change and get along with all types of people, you could be headed home much sooner than expected.

From my own experience, research, and interviews with expatriates and international recruiters, I've identified 13 success indicators for living and working abroad. Before you pack your bags and hop on the next flight to your dream destination abroad, take a few minutes to consider how you measure up in each.

Adaptability

Adaptability, or flexibility, is one of the most essential skills for success overseas. How quickly and easily can you change course when something unexpected happens? Think of a Dilbertlike scenario for just a minute. Your boss is considering a new business site and wants you to do a cost analysis of the proposal. You and your project team have just spent the better part of the last month working up some figures. You're excited to show your boss the numbers that indicate that the project is a great opportunity. Unfortunately, your boss is no longer interested in the project and tells you to scrap the plan. How do you handle that? You might know how you'd react at home. But what happens when you're in another country and facing other challenges at the same time?

If you're too fixed or rigid in your needs and expectations, you'll have a difficult time adjusting to cultural differences and, consequently, working abroad. Unless you demonstrate your ability to go with the flow in your new location, you may find yourself experiencing severe culture shock, which can paralyze your ability to get the job done.

Acceptance of Differences

Ask yourself: Is it really OK for others to have different values and beliefs than your own? What happens when these values and belief systems collide, as they undoubtedly will? You may be able to tolerate differences on an intellectual level, but how will you feel and react on an emotional level? How are you going to feel on a blistering summer day in Mumbai, when you've been patiently standing in line waiting your turn to cash a check, people keep cutting in front of you, and the cashier does nothing about it? It's one thing to tolerate differences; it's another thing to be truly open and accepting of them. If you find it difficult to be nonjudgmental about differences, whether they be about personal beliefs, communication styles, or values, you may also find it hard to deal with differences at work. When this happens, you cannot be as effective as you need to be in achieving your business goals and objectives. Accepting other people as they are, rather than trying to change their values or beliefs, frees up a tremendous amount of energy. You and those you interact with can agree to disagree, while staying focused on your common objectives.

The process necessary to get a job done, including how long it will take to get results, may be less clear abroad than at home. Employees who speak English as a second language might nod affirmatively in response to your question, "Do you understand what I mean?" Only later will you learn that the nods simply meant that they heard you, not that they understood you—at least not exactly. If you trust yourself and your ability to do what it takes to succeed, you'll minimize the frustration you feel when you encounter cultural differences.

The Three Ps: A Positive Attitude, Patience, Perseverance

A positive attitude, patience, perseverance—these "three Ps" will play an important role in your success abroad. If you are a positive person, you'll more easily roll with the punches when things don't go the way you've planned. You'll also find it easier to develop relationships with others who can offer support as you go through the inevitable phases of culture shock. A positive attitude allows you to keep things in perspective and not let annoying situations escalate into major problems.

Patience, too, is indeed a virtue when working abroad. In mainstream North American culture, we're used to moving fast. Time is money, after all. You're probably used to getting what you want when you want it because you've learned, sometimes the hard way, how to get things done. Yet working overseas can try even the most patient of people, and it often requires a great capacity to wait. If you plan on living in a country that lacks an efficient infrastructure, you'll need even more patience. Maybe restaurant service takes longer than you'd like. Maybe you can't walk as fast as normal because of the crowds of people, or you can't read easily at night because you never know when the electricity will fail. Can you live with the fact that business decisions may have to go through several layers of employees, not just management, before you get the answers you need?

Those who succeed in international assignments are also able to persevere—to get their jobs done despite unexpected obstacles and challenges along the way. Confident in their experience and competent in their expertise, they are able to maneuver effectively to achieve their desired goals. They stay the course when their efforts do not pay off immediately.

Ability to Communicate across Cultures

Have you ever had difficulty expressing yourself in a second language or understanding a second-language learner? Do you remember how you felt? You probably experienced feelings of discomfort and maybe embarrassment.

To reach the goal of communication, which is mutual understanding, you have to find your way through the maze of language and cultural differences. How well can you get your point across to those who may speak a different language or come from a different cultural background? Remember that using gestures can get you into trouble. When I was traveling in Brazil, people would ask how I was doing. I'd smile and flash the ubiquitous OK sign, using my index finger and thumb. I quickly discovered that instead of signaling "everything's all right," I was really making a terribly vulgar and obscene gesture. When you see a look of shock and horror on the faces of people around you, it's usually a good indication that maybe something is wrong with a particular gesture.

Ability to Fail

In his pioneering work, *Survival Kit for Overseas Living*, L. Robert Kohls identified the ability to fail as one of the most critical qualities for success abroad. Perhaps you were selected for an overseas assignment because of your high-performance track record. You may not know what it means to fail. If you expect to achieve that same level of performance quickly when working abroad, you may be sadly disappointed. You have to allow for the possibility that it will take you longer to achieve your customary level of performance overseas. This fact can cause a great deal of frustration if you have been a high performer in your career until now. By entertaining the possibility that you may *not* progress as quickly as you'd like in your job abroad, you can take steps to alleviate the impact of the occasional failure on your self-esteem and future career opportunities.

Sense of Humor

The ability to see the humor in frustrating situations allows you to keep the things that go wrong in perspective. You have to be able to laugh at yourself, and your own mistakes, to survive your international experience. This isn't always easy when you're feeling embarrassed because of something you said or inadvertently did. In the long run, however, humor is the key to maintaining your sanity and balance. Without it, your journeys abroad might not be adventures as much as hardships, and your stay will be much less enjoyable and fruitful.

Self-Reliance

You will have a much harder time adjusting to working abroad if you are easily intimidated by unfamiliar situations. To succeed, you will often need to depend upon yourself rather than others to get information, create a comfortable living arrangement, find your way home when you get lost, forge friendships, and so forth. On a teaching assignment in Egypt, I had great admiration for one of the other women in our small group. She was 63 years old and thought nothing of going off by herself each day to see and do exactly what she wanted, without waiting to see if any of the rest of us were so inclined. She would come back at the end of the day carrying fabulous gifts and filled with wondrous stories of the people she had met along the way. If she ever found herself in intimidating situations, she never let on.

It's normal to feel frustrated when things don't work the way you want them to, but what counts is how you deal with that frustration. You can expect challenges in communication, transportation, and other daily occurrences overseas. If you have a hard time dealing with those kinds of challenges, then working abroad is probably not for you.

Curiosity

The more curious you are about others' lifestyles, customs, and beliefs, the more likely you are to learn and develop an appreciation of another culture. By expressing an active interest in another person's cultural point of view, you will find it easier to build relationships and acquire international friends who can be very instrumental in helping you achieve your goals.

Outgoingness

If you're outgoing, it will be easier to make friends and ask for help when you need it. If you're willing to risk making mistakes when speaking another language, for instance, you'll acculturate faster than someone who is more introverted. Of course, you may be a reserved person by nature and still succeed in another culture. But success might take longer.

You may find that while you are somewhat quiet in your own culture, once abroad, you assume a different persona. As one of my workshop participants stated, "You know, here I'm pretty quiet, but when I'm in Mexico, I'm really a different person!" That's fine, but be wary of trying to "go native," which may be seen as disrespectful or just plain silly. Remember when Dan Rather donned Afghan garb during his report from Afghanistan? He was quickly ridiculed by the media as "Gunga Dan."

People prefer to do business with those who are friendly and approachable. Your open, friendly attitude maximizes opportunities for gaining the trust of others who can help you get what you want.

Motivation

When you are motivated to perform at your best, it's easier to cope with difficult situations and see them through to resolution no matter what it takes. Motivation is a desirable trait to have when working abroad, especially if you are working for an organization based back home, since you may find yourself communicating less often with the mother ship than you'd like. When you're motivated, you can get through most everything.

Trust

If you're working in an unfamiliar environment, in which you don't know all the rules of doing business and getting things done, you'll need to inspire and develop trust with others fairly quickly. A colleague once observed that there are two kinds of people: those who trust someone unreservedly unless or until the person does something to break the trust, and those who believe a person has to earn their trust before they give it. It pays to be cautious with people you don't know well, but sooner or later you'll need to take a leap of faith. You'll have to put your trust in someone you may not know as well as you'd like because of the language and cultural differences between you.

Acculturation

Acculturation is the ability to live in another culture with relative ease. A person who is acculturated is aware of cultural differences and their impact on self and others and has learned how to manage these differences effectively. Yes, it's hard to live in conditions that, by your standards, are unsanitary, overpopulated, noisy, and without many of the modern conveniences that you depend on. Yet shielding yourself from uncomfortable experiences will give you an inaccurate picture of what it's really like to live in some other countries. By sanitizing your experience, you might be lucky enough to avoid an illness or two, but you could also miss out on much of the local flavor and color that ultimately enriches your appreciation for what you do have.

In truth, it's unrealistic to think you can avoid having unpleasant experiences while abroad. Try as you might, troubles often have a way of catching up with you. I made sure to drink bottled water while living in Cairo, but ultimately suffered the same fate as others in my group who didn't. I soon discovered why, in the kitchen one day, when I came upon one of the young women with whom I lived. She was kindly refilling my water bottles with tap water and had no idea why I wouldn't simply drink from the tap myself. Oh well. While I would have preferred not to have had that particular experience, I survived to tell the story—and, in all likelihood, you will, too. One's level of acculturation is individual, of course, and it pays to explore your own level of comfort in deciding where you want to live and work abroad and under what conditions.

Cultural Understanding

To truly understand another culture, it's important to put yourself in another person's place as much as possible. This means deliberately putting yourself in uncomfortable situations. When I first considered a career as a speaker in cross-cultural communications, I set up an informational interview with an African American executive. She told me I needed exposure in the black community and that I needed to put myself in potentially uncomfortable situations in which I would be the only white person present. She was right. Or, in the words of Clark Roberts, a professional speaker on the issue of visually impaired diversity, "We just have to get comfortable with being uncomfortable." Without a greater understanding of another person's values, beliefs, and communication styles, behavior can be misinterpreted and misunderstood.

WHAT CAN I DO, RIGHT NOW, TO INCREASE MY CHANCES FOR SUCCESS?

First evaluate how you rate on the 13 success indicators discussed in the preceding pages. Then take the following steps in planning a move overseas:

Ask Yourself: "Why Am I Doing It?"

If you're seeking work abroad to escape unpleasant circumstances at home, keep in mind that you may only end up aggravating an already unhappy situation. The Foreign Legion notwithstanding, you can run but you can't hide—and this fact is true on a global scale as well. Don't look to work abroad as a way out; look at it as a way *toward* something that you truly want to do for increased personal and professional fulfillment.

Having said all that, I do know of one former colleague who went through a messy divorce in the States and decided to work abroad, mostly to get away. He went on to meet his next wife during his overseas assignment, and they came back to the United States to raise their family. As far as I know, they are still happily married. So it's not that you can't find happiness on the heels of a bad situation at home, but you can't count on it. Even worse, you may exacerbate an already untenable emotional situation with the additional cultural adjustments and sense of isolation you may feel while living abroad.

Involve the Entire Family

In the 1995 survey among members of the NFTC, respondents cited family problems as the second most significant factor (64 percent) contributing to failed international assignments. Yet a 1998 report on global relocation trends found that 89 percent of married expatriates go on assignment with their spouses, and 55 percent of expatriates bring children. Companies may help you find a place to live and schools for your children. But after that, you're on your own.

Typically, the family member who gets the global assignment has built-in support at work, whereas his or her partner rarely has a job or the support that goes with it. How is your partner going to feel if you get an international job that requires long work hours and travel, while he or she is left behind to manage the home and children? How do your children feel about uprooting themselves and leaving their friends? What if you don't have any children? Will your partner feel even more isolated and alone in unfamiliar surroundings?

Happily, these are issues that can be resolved. When you involve your entire family in your plans to live and work abroad, it can build a sense of excitement and ownership. And if your partner or children plan to accompany you on your overseas assignment, the family will need to tackle issues head-on before going global.

Increase Your Language and Cultural Fluency

Before you can find out whether or not you'll need to speak a second language in your international job, you have to know what type of work you want to do. From there, you'll need to know the particulars of the overseas assignment you receive. Even if it's not a job requirement, second-language fluency can give you a competitive edge when all other factors between two candidates are equal. There's no question that you will have an easier time working and adjusting to life abroad if you speak the native language and have some cultural understanding of the host population, whether or not you actually need fluency to perform your job successfully.

If your foreign-language skills are a bit rusty, have your second-language fluency level evaluated by a professional. Contact a private language institute or the testing office at your local community college or university. Berlitz Language Centers, for example, offer a foreign-language testing assessment based on the Foreign Service Institute Level System. You'll want to take a language exam that will measure your spoken, written, and reading fluency. The test results will allow you to speak accurately about your second-language fluency, rather than guessing whether you are at the beginning, intermediate, or advanced level.

You don't want to run the risk of overestimating your second-language ability and ending up in an embarrassing situation. For example, one prospective teacher stated on his resume that he was fluent in Farsi, not knowing that the administrator conducting the interview had spent several years in Iran and was herself fluent in Farsi. When she attempted to communicate in the language, the applicant was unable to converse, and an awkward silence followed. He didn't get the job.

Network Like Crazy

Join and become active in international professional organizations. When you do, you'll learn about current hiring trends and practices, emerging international destinations for job seekers, and specific job opportunities abroad.

Hopefully, you haven't burned bridges with former associates; you never know when someone you knew five or more years ago can help you find work abroad. Yes, it takes a lot of time and effort to maintain contact with people you've worked with or met through professional organizations in the past. Yet this time and effort is well spent and can reap significant benefits.

Strengthen Your Credentials

While investigating overseas work opportunities, take courses or do volunteer work that can make you more desirable to an international employer. In addition to increasing your language and cultural fluency, improve your computer, management, and interpersonal skills.

EXPLORATION EXERCISES

The following exercises will help you assess your chances for success overseas and visualize your overseas employment. Do as many exercises as you need to focus your global job search. I know you'd rather cut to the chase and have an international job assignment just drop into your lap, but it doesn't usually happen that dramatically. So trust me on this. Work on your personal mission now. You'll be glad you did. Going through the preliminary steps is essential not just in finding work abroad, but also in finding work that you find inspiring and fulfilling.

Self-Assessment Test

This personality assessment tool will help you determine your potential for international success. Read each of the statements below and rate yourself on a scale of 1 (No) to 5 (Yes). Be as open and honest as possible and cite specific examples to confirm your impressions. The higher your score, the greater your chances for success.

Indicators for Overseas Success

I can adapt to unusual or unexpected situations.

1	2	3	4	5
No		Sometimes		Yes

Example: _____

_____

I communicate and interact effectively with other people, despite differences in viewpoints, values, or beliefs.

1	2	3	4	5
No		Sometimes		Yes

Example: _____

_____

It's OK for other people to have different values and beliefs from my own.

1	2	3	4	5
No		Sometimes		Yes

Example: _____

_____

I perform my job effectively despite changes, challenges, or delays.

1	2	3	4	5
No		Sometimes		Yes

Example: _____

_____

I have experienced failure professionally and/or personally.

1	2	3	4	5
No		Sometimes		Yes

Example: _____

_____

I can see the humor in difficult or uncomfortable situations and can laugh at my own mistakes.

1	2	3	4	5
No		Sometimes		Yes

Example: _____

_____

I am self-reliant and not often intimidated by unfamiliar situations.

1	2	3	4	5
No		Sometimes		Yes

Example: _____

_____

I am curious about other people's cultures, customs, and beliefs.

1	2	3	4	5
No		Sometimes		Yes

Example: _____

_____

I look for opportunities to make new friends wherever I go.

1	2	3	4	5
No		Sometimes		Yes

Example: _____

_____

I am self-motivated and require little direction in my work.

1	2	3	4	5
No		Sometimes		Yes

Example: _____

_____

I know what kind of work I want to do overseas.

1	2	3	4	5
No		Sometimes		Yes

Example: _____

_____

I belong to and am active in professional international organizations.

1	2	3	4	5
No		Sometimes		Yes

Example: _____

_____

I have the necessary academic credentials and experience in the type of work I want to do overseas.

1	2	3	4	5
No		Sometimes		Yes

Example: _____

_____

I maintain contact with former coworkers and business colleagues.

1	2	3	4	5
No		Sometimes		Yes

Example: _____

_____

I speak the language and have some cultural understanding of the host country in which I want to work.

1	2	3	4	5
No		Sometimes		Yes

Example: _____

_____

My partner and family expect to accompany me overseas and have realistic expectations of living abroad.

1	2	3	4	5
No		Sometimes		Yes

Example: _____

_____

I am looking for an international job to enhance my professional development and my life and not to escape or avoid unhappy circumstances in my life here.

1	2	3	4	5
No		Sometimes		Yes

Example: _____

_____

I know where I want to live abroad and have researched business and social norms there.

1	2	3	4	5
No		Sometimes		Yes

Example: _____

_____

I know the type of organization for which I'd like to work and how my skills might benefit such an organization.

1	2	3	4	5
No		Sometimes		Yes

Example: _____

_____

I have a good understanding of my host organization's philosophy and culture, required professional credentials, salary standards, and benefits package.

1	2	3	4	5
No		Sometimes		Yes

Example: _____

_____

Indicators for Difficulties in Working Overseas

Read each of the questions below and rate yourself on a scale of 1 (No) to 5 (Yes). The higher your score, the more difficulty you might have working overseas.

I get impatient if expected results take longer than planned.

1	2	3	4	5
No		Sometimes		Yes

Example: _____

_____

I set high performance standards for myself and am upset when my performance does not meet my expectations.

1	2	3	4	5
No		Sometimes		Yes

Example: _____

_____

I find it hard to accept poverty, and I do my best to avoid poor areas whenever possible.

1	2	3	4	5
No		Sometimes		Yes

Example: _____

_____

I become frustrated easily in unfamiliar situations.

1	2	3	4	5
No		Sometimes		Yes

Example: _____

_____

It's sometimes hard for me to accept other people's attitudes and beliefs.

1	2	3	4	5
No		Sometimes		Yes

Example: _____

_____

Let your test results be a map of what you've done so far and what you need to do next to reach your dream of working abroad. Keep your end goal in sight and divide it into sub-goals to make the process more manageable and less overwhelming.

Visualization Exercises

While some of you may find these next five exercises a bit "New Agey" (and you know who you are), these techniques can help you tap into your subconscious and have proven helpful to many who have used them.

Programmed Visualization   A programmed visualization is the deliberate attempt to create the outcome you desire using the power of your mind. When you know what your goal is, visualization helps you "see" your dream as reality. Here's how it works.

You can either make a tape recording in your own voice or ask someone to read to you the following visualization exercise. It should be read slowly and purposefully to allow you time to visualize your responses to the questions. The clearer you can actually visualize yourself working abroad, the more motivated you will be to take specific steps to make your dream a reality and the more likely you are to attract resources to help you get what you want. Take a moment to get comfortably seated. Now listen to the following:

Close your eyes and relax your body. Stretch to release any tension in your body. Take as long as you need to feel completely relaxed and comfortable. Breathe slowly, deeply, and evenly. Slowly inhale and exhale for several minutes. Allow the chatter inside your head to slowly subside as you concentrate only on your breathing. When you feel completely relaxed and comfortable, begin to picture yourself in your ideal international job.

Picture yourself doing exactly the kind of work you want to do overseas. Use all of your senses to capture how you feel doing what you want to do. See yourself at the start of your day and then as you arrive at your workplace. Hear the conversations in which you are engaged or listening to. Feel the fabric of the clothes you are wearing and smell the air around you. Pay close attention to your emotions as you spend time holding this image of your perfect work situation abroad.

As you open your eyes, stay with this image of working successfully abroad. Take a few moments now to capture the essence of your visualization in writing. Describe your ideal international assignment in vivid, specific detail, using all your senses to make your vision come alive. What are you doing exactly? What does the situation look, feel, sound, and taste like to you? What does working abroad give you that you don't have now? How does it enhance your life? Keep this written description where you can refer to it later.

I first used this technique several years ago to visualize my dream job in international relations. I came across my written description a year or two after I had gotten my desired employment. I was amazed at how closely my written description matched the position I ended up taking.

Your Dream Employment Ad   Using the information from your programmed visualization, write your own dream international job advertisement. What should the ad say to make you respond, "Yes! That's me exactly. That's my job! It has my name on it!"

Include such information as your title, job responsibilities, credentials and experience required, amount of travel required, type of organization, salary range, location, and anything else that tells you that this is a job ready-made for you to fill.

Affirmation Statements   From the detailed description of your dream international assignment, you can also create affirmation statements to reinforce the power of your visualization. To be most effective, an affirmation should describe a goal as if it's already a reality. It should be a positive, declarative statement in the first person, present tense, and should express an emotion.

Here is an affirmation about my goal of getting published: "I am happily and easily getting published for the greatest good of all concerned." OK, I admit, I had to work hard at the part about "easily getting published," but, as you can see, I was successful in my efforts.

Treasure Mapping   A treasure map is a photo collage that represents your vision of your dream overseas assignment. It can be a very effective tool for actualizing your vision, so be careful what you wish for, as the old adage goes, because you just might get it.

Look through magazines to find pictures that symbolize or show what you want your life and work abroad to look like. Paste the pictures on a large poster board and place it where you can see it at least once a day. If you'd prefer to make your own pictures, gather several large sheets of paper and some colored markers and draw your own dream international lifestyle. This treasure map will serve as an effective reminder of your dream and will help focus your energies on taking the steps to make it happen.

Receptive Visualization This visualization exercise is a brief example of what you can do to begin getting in touch with the type of global position that feels right for you.

Close your eyes and relax your body. Stretch to release any tension. Take as long as you need to feel completely relaxed and comfortable. Breathe slowly, deeply, and evenly. Slowly inhale and exhale for several minutes. Allow the chatter inside your head to slowly subside as you concentrate only on your breathing. When you feel completely relaxed and comfortable, begin to picture yourself in your ideal international job.

What kind of work are you doing? Do you have a title? If so, what is it? What exactly are your job responsibilities? What language are you speaking? What type of clothes are you wearing? Who are you talking to? What are you talking about? Are you working alone or with other people? If you are working with other people, who are they? What type of organization are you working for? What do you see around you? What kind of space are you working in? What does it look like? What sounds do you hear around you? How many people work for this organization? What range of salary and benefits are you receiving? Where in the world are you?

When you are ready to come back to the present, gradually open your eyes and continue sitting comfortably for a few more moments. How are you feeling right now? If you are feeling positive about what you saw in your mind's eye, it's a good indication that you're on the right track in your international employment goal. If not, it's worth spending more time to see where any negative feelings might be coming from.

On paper, describe your ideal international assignment in vivid and specific detail. Use all your senses to make your vision come alive. What does it *look, feel, sound,* and *taste* like?

Food for Thought

Write brief answers to the following questions. When you are finished, look for any patterns in your responses. What picture is emerging that tells you where you might want to live abroad?

- What kind of restaurants do I like?
- What kind of food do I like to cook or eat?
- When do I prefer to eat my meals?
- What kind of music do I like to listen to?
- What type of foreign films do I enjoy the most?
- What foreign languages do I enjoy listening to?
- What foreign language do I speak?
- What foreign language would I like to learn?
- How do I like to dress for work?
- In what kind of climate do I do my best work?
- What do I like to do outside of work in my free time?
- Where have I enjoyed spending my vacations in the past?

If you find that you enjoy having dinner later in the evening, head to Spain, where you'll have lots of people to keep you company. If you discovered that you'd rather eat at Perkins or Denny's more than anywhere else, you might not want to stray too far from home. If you vacationed once in Kuala Lumpur and had a terrible experience, you might not want to go back there to work.

Sentence Completion

Nathaniel Branden, noted psychologist in the field of self-esteem, is known for his use of sentence completions to help patients uncover their innermost thoughts and feelings. You can use a similar technique to discover what kind of work you want to do abroad and where you most want to live.

Complete the following sentences. Write quickly, without analyzing or censoring your responses. Spend time with each statement and write at least 10 different endings for each.

- If I could live anywhere in the world...
- If I could do any kind of work abroad...
- If I could work for the organization of my choice...
- If I could speak a second language...

- If I could learn more about another culture...

When you're finished, take a look at what you wrote. What did you discover about yourself and your dream of living and working abroad?

WHAT WILL YOU DO NEXT?

Before moving on to the next chapter, take these steps toward reaching your dream of living and working abroad. Remember to set specific, measurable, and realistic goals and a deadline for completing them. Here are a few places to start:

- Develop a specific goal for working abroad. It should include a hoped-for job title and responsibilities, type of organization, location, length of stay, and your motivation for relocation.
- Complete as many exercises in this chapter as are helpful.
- Set up a time with a partner or family members to discuss your dream of working overseas. Work together to create a family plan for going global.
- Develop strategies to increase your competencies. To increase your cultural understanding, for example, read resources on cultural differences, attend workshops on diversity awareness, and ask for help.
- Investigate classes and volunteer work that will strengthen your credentials for working overseas.
- Take a second-language proficiency test.

2

Get the Facts—
Research!

*In order that the world may have a little more knowledge, that
it may build on what it knows instead of on what it thinks.*
—Apsley Cherry-Garrard, polar explorer

What kinds of foreign assignments are available and how can you find
them? How can you get creative in your job search? This chapter will help
answer these and other questions. You will learn how to find work you love
in a job market that makes fulfilling international employment possible.

TRENDS IN INTERNATIONAL HIRING

Increasing access to technology, political changes in Eastern Europe, the
European Unification Act, and NAFTA (North American Free Trade
Agreement)—all have paved the way for expanding international commerce. And that expansion is taking place in small to mid-sized firms, not
just in large companies. This is good news for international job seekers
because small firms can often put you to work overseas sooner than can
larger, more established businesses. And senior managers and executives
are not the only ones being hired for international jobs. As globalization
becomes increasingly important to business revenues, the number of foreign work assignments will continue to grow.

On the down side for international job seekers, some companies want
to employ expatriates for only short-term assignments—to establish

business overseas until day-to-day operations can be handed off to local nationals. It's clearly less expensive for companies to hire local nationals than to move employees abroad at high salaries. Yet employing workers abroad for short-term assignments may limit a company's effectiveness in nurturing critical business relationships. Some companies, such as Boeing Corporation, are taking a second look at the length of foreign assignments. They are realizing the benefit of extending expatriates' contracts in order to build long-term business relationships in host countries and to maintain global competitiveness.

WHERE ARE THE JOB OPPORTUNITIES ABROAD?

According to the latest figures compiled by Windham International and the National Foreign Trade Council, the majority of those seeking international work are assigned to the United Kingdom, the United States, and Hong Kong. The same survey cited China, Brazil, and India as emerging new locations for international assignments.

A 1996 Commerce Department report, *The Big Emerging Markets,* identified the following promising markets for U.S. exports and investment abroad:
- The Americas (Argentina, Brazil, Mexico)
- Southeast Asia (Singapore, Indonesia, Thailand, Malaysia, the Philippines, Brunei, Vietnam)
- The Chinese Economic Area (China, Hong Kong, Taiwan)
- India
- South Korea
- Europe (Poland)
- The Middle East (Turkey)
- Africa (South Africa)

While these markets were cited because of their recent economic reforms and increasing market stability, it's evident from the recent downturn in the Asian economy and the devaluation of Brazil's real, for example, that many of these so-called promising markets remain extremely volatile, as do our relations with many of their governments. The truth is, opportunities change, and while it's worth your time to explore untapped

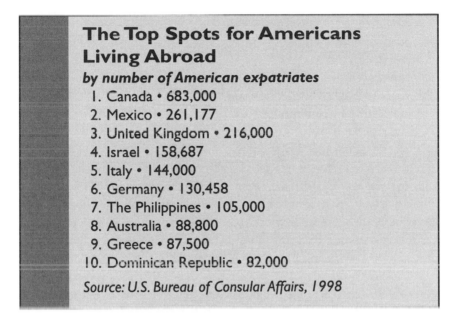

The Top Spots for Americans Living Abroad
by number of American expatriates
1. Canada • 683,000
2. Mexico • 261,177
3. United Kingdom • 216,000
4. Israel • 158,687
5. Italy • 144,000
6. Germany • 130,458
7. The Philippines • 105,000
8. Australia • 88,800
9. Greece • 87,500
10. Dominican Republic • 82,000

Source: U.S. Bureau of Consular Affairs, 1998

markets when considering job opportunities abroad, always remain flexible to the hidden opportunities just over the horizon.

WHAT KINDS OF INTERNATIONAL JOBS ARE AVAILABLE?

Particular jobs and industries are traditionally associated with positions overseas. Here are a few of them:

- bilingual education
- broadcasting and journalism
- business and banking
- community development
- consulting
- economic development
- environmental work
- foreign service
- health care and relief efforts
- high technology

- importing and exporting
- international law
- international trade
- military service
- teaching English as a foreign language
- translating and interpreting
- travel and tourism
- travel writing and photography

If you were to stop at this list, though, you would be greatly limiting your overseas job opportunities. Remember, most international jobs have a domestic counterpart. In many cases, the work you do abroad will be similar to, if not the same as, the work you do at home. Think about opportunities in engineering, advertising, domestic service, entertainment, health care, and manufacturing. The possibilities, really, are unlimited.

Consider, too, which industries are predicted to grow overseas in the years ahead. The U.S. Department of Commerce lists five major industries that represent the greatest job opportunities in the "Big Emerging Markets." These industries are transportation, information, health care, energy, and finance.

Why these five? Because of the need to develop new commercial infrastructures to support the emerging markets' growing economies. The Commerce Department expects that "the [Big Emerging Markets] will double their share of world imports . . . rising to 38 percent by 2010 from 19 percent in 1994. . . . From Seoul to Bombay, plans call for well over $1 trillion in infrastructure projects in the next 10 years—in energy exploration and generation, airports and air traffic systems, phones and satellites, hospitals and health care services, auto and auto parts production, banking and insurance, and environmental clean-up."

In response, the International Trade Administration has targeted worldwide development projects as follows:

Power generation, oil, and gas: 35.0%

Transportation and infrastructure: 29.6%

Aerospace: 5.7%

Computer and telecommunications: 3.8%

Environmental: 3.4%

Other (defense, services, etc.): 22.6%

For those seeking employment in emerging markets, the need for technical experts in each of these areas, as well as the need for managers and marketing, sales, and communication specialists, will provide significant opportunities in the decades ahead.

WHAT ORGANIZATIONS EMPLOY WORKERS ABROAD?

The Federal Government

With more than 50 separate agencies doing business overseas, the U.S. federal government is one of the largest employers of international workers. The government offers a variety of opportunities in the military, economic, and social sectors, including such positions as foreign service officer, information specialist, administrator, and business development specialist. Federal agencies that employ personnel abroad include the Foreign Service of the Department of State, the United States Information Agency (USIA), the Agency for International Development (AID), the Peace Corps, and the Central Intelligence Agency (CIA).

To find out about jobs with the federal government abroad, you can contact individual agencies for their job requirements and application information or check the latest edition of the *Federal Jobs Digest* for current listings. In a recent issue, I counted approximately 50 advertised overseas positions, in such countries as Saudi Arabia, Greece, Iceland, the United Kingdom, and Spain. Consider, too, the government's Office of Personnel Management, which hires nationwide for the Civil Service and posts job announcements at Job Information Centers in most states. Many of the government's large domestic agencies, such as the Department of Commerce, have international divisions that you may want to investigate for job openings—even though most of the work is done in the United States.

Educational Institutions

If you are an educator at heart, you might consider teaching English as a foreign language abroad. It's one of the fastest and easiest ways to secure foreign employment. Many positions are available through private and public institutions, as well as the federal government. While it is not always necessary to have a certificate or an advanced degree in English as a Foreign Language (EFL), you will be in a more competitive position and command a higher salary if you have one. Browsing through a recent copy of the *International Employment Gazette,* I found many EFL opportunities available in Japan, Korea, and China.

Teaching overseas is not limited to those wishing to teach English as a foreign language, however. The Department of Defense employs elementary and secondary school teachers at its schools overseas, in order to provide an American-style education to dependents of active military and civilian personnel. International School Services (ISS) recruits teachers for American schools worldwide (excluding Department of Defense schools), to provide education to children of expatriates. If you are an assistant or associate professor with an advanced degree, you may also find teaching opportunities abroad at colleges and universities.

International Public Organizations

International public organizations include the United Nations, the World Bank, the International Monetary Fund, the World Health Organization, UNICEF, and UNESCO. As you might suspect, these organizations are among the most difficult to join as a new hire. The positions that are offered tend to go to those with specialized degrees and a great depth and breadth of experience in their fields. One way to gain entry into international organizations is as a consultant, which leads us to the next section.

International Consulting Firms

There are two approaches you might take as an independent consultant seeking international work. First, you can contact an organization or agency directly to offer your services. Mary Kay is an example. She is a professional speaker who often accompanies her husband on business trips around the world. Before leaving for Thailand, she contacted a group of American businesses operating in Bangkok and sent out proposals for a presentation. She received several offers in response and ended up giving a very successful presentation to a group of Thai women.

With the second approach, you subcontract with a consulting firm that needs people to manage worldwide projects. For example, Winston

International Employment Intrigue

I once received a postcard from a former dorm mate who had joined the CIA after graduating from college with a degree in accounting. The postcard simply read, "You'll never guess where I am." I never did, and I never heard from him again. For all I know, he was just on vacation, but the mystique of "missions impossible" surrounding the CIA and other such agencies dies hard. Even *Writer's Digest* spoofed the organization some years back, in a contest asking readers to come up with a better slogan for the CIA than *The World Is Our Business*. The writer suggested "We Love to Spy and It Shows" and "Join the CIA. We Can't Tell You Why."

had developed a strong track record as an independent contractor with a national training organization. When the company expanded its programs into Australia and South Africa, Winston jumped at the chance to deliver his presentations overseas.

Many consulting positions abroad fall into the areas of planning, management, and engineering. As in the United States, international firms require experienced contractors who can come in and get the job done on time and on budget.

U.S. Multinationals

U.S. multinationals may be small, mid-sized, or large American companies with operations abroad. Multinationals operate in industries such as banking, manufacturing, transportation, oil, food and agriculture, travel and leisure, high-tech communications, finance, and insurance. They include companies like Federal Express, Merrill Lynch, IBM, Coca-Cola, American Express, Ford, Mobil, Proctor & Gamble, McDonald's, and the Marriott Corporation. While there is no one surefire way to break into a position in a U.S. multinational, it helps to have a background in business, management, or communications, depending, of course, on the position.

Foreign-owned Companies

Unless you are already living or working overseas, or have contacts who can refer you to specific individuals at companies, it may be difficult to get hired by a foreign-owned company. One approach is to contact foreign companies that have offices in the United States and to get more information before deciding whether or not to pursue a position with them abroad. Ask for company literature and inquire about job opportunities, qualifications required, and application procedures.

Nonprofit and Volunteer Agencies

Nonprofit and volunteer organizations working overseas often specialize in disaster relief, health care, community planning, or agricultural development. Some are affiliated with religious institutions, but many others are not. Among the most well-known agencies are CARE, Save the Children Federation, Catholic Relief Services, World Vision Relief, and the Salvation Army.

If you have limited work experience, your initial job opportunities with such organizations may be unpaid or minimally paid. However, administrative posts with such agencies are generally paid positions and are often quite competitive.

HOW CAN I FIND INTERNATIONAL JOBS?

Even when you know what kind of position you want, where you want to live abroad, and where the worldwide employment opportunities are, how do you zero in on a specific job? Whether you are seeking an ecological adventure on the Amazon or semiretirement in the Azores, you need to know how to take advantage of unexpected opportunities and tap into existing employment resources.

I happened to be looking for new worlds to conquer when my company received a flyer advertising teaching positions in Cairo. While I hadn't been thinking of Egypt in particular, it wasn't too long before my bags were packed. Here are some other stories of successful expatriates:

"My international jobs have come from people seeing me in action and referrals," says Marie, a translator and interpreter. She began by taking on small local jobs at first, both independently and through agencies. She then received additional certification from the ATA (American Translators' Association) to bolster her credentials. Gradually, she began to take on larger projects, and she became known for her competence. A request by Boeing Corporation to interpret at a technical conference was the springboard into her present-day niche as a technical translator and interpreter for corporations and for ISO (International Standards Organization) conferences. Yet Marie did not gain her expertise overnight. She recognized the opportunity to develop depth in a specific area, and she began her specialized education in technical terminology.

Even if you're an experienced professional, you can't benefit from your track record if other people don't know what you have to offer. Like Marie, you must find work that increases your exposure. Seek out opportunities for showcasing your talent. Write articles for trade journals. Offer to speak at local business organizations. Create your own Web site. Get known for what you do. Be willing, too, to invest in your career through continuing education. For Marie, this meant acquiring a new technical vocabulary outside her area of expertise—a considerable investment in time and energy that bore handsome dividends.

Les, another success story, had an advanced degree from Thunderbird University, which specializes in international business. He also studied Japanese following his discharge from the military. When Les began researching overseas jobs, he came across information on a freight-forwarding company. In reviewing its annual report, he discovered that the company had opened an office in London and was expanding into other global markets. The company offered Les a position in his home-town of Chicago, which he took in hopes that he would be able to go overseas when the right opportunity, specifically a position in Japan, presented itself. Six months later, when the company was ready to open an office in Japan, Les was tapped for the position of manager. His international career continued upon his return to the United States. He became friends with a Korean graduate student, and together they developed a business selling clock oscillators to wholesale distributors and, later, to original equipment manufacturers throughout the world. "I took a gamble and it paid off," says Les, about his overseas work experience.

Just as Les researched company literature and learned what he wanted to know by reviewing the freight company's annual report, you, too, will want to do your homework. Get factual information and learn to read between the lines. You may never gather all the information you'd like to have before making a decision, but be certain that you have researched the market as thoroughly as possible. Like Les, you may be taking a gamble, but what job—international or domestic, employment or entrepreneurship—doesn't involve an element of risk?

You may be reading Marie's and Les's profiles with just a hint of envy. You're probably wishing one of their opportunities could become available to you. It can. For anyone willing to invest the time and energy—whether or not you speak a second language or have a degree in international management—there are unlimited possibilities when it comes to finding an international job. The key is knowing where to look and knowing what to do with the information you discover.

WHERE TO LOOK

Here are some suggestions on where to begin your global job search, whether you're seeking employment or a business venture; part-time, full-time, temporary, permanent, short-term, or long-term work. Don't rely on only one or two of these resources—use them in combination to get as much access and exposure to international employment opportunities as possible. (See the Appendix for additional recommendations about international employment resources.)

Your Current Employer

Start close to home in your international employment search—you might be surprised at what you find. Many employers would rather hire someone from within the firm for a position overseas than risk the investment on an unknown staff member. A proven track record and demonstrated loyalty to your company can give you an inside edge when an international position turns up.

A friend of mine was reluctant to relocate to another American city in his position as a commercial insurance underwriter. Then, the company asked if he wanted to live and work in Argentina instead. Though my friend ultimately decided against the offer, his story shows that international job opportunities may be hidden within your own organization. But you won't necessarily find out what they are if you don't ask or keep your ear to the ground. Increase your visibility and do whatever you can to keep in the loop as new business opportunities develop within your company. That way, you will be among the first to know about and be considered for that overseas assignment.

The Public Library

The public library is your greatest resource for printed information to assist in your global job search. At the library, you can find out how Montevideo got its name, read what Egyptians eat for breakfast, learn why dragons are used in Chinese celebrations, see the latest fashion trends in magazines from Brazil and Italy, explore the design of the Taj Mahal, investigate the story of mapping, brush up on your Greek and Slavic languages, discover how to close a business deal in Budapest, and learn whether to bow or shake hands in Japan. In fact, perhaps the library was where you first felt the stirrings of wanderlust, as you came upon some of the many hidden treasures within.

It pays to cultivate a close working relationship with your reference librarian. He or she is generally more than happy to assist in your quest for information, often the more exotic or esoteric the better, and can save you time in your research. A good reference librarian loves a research challenge. He or she can refer you to directories you didn't know existed and can help you through the maze of confusing indexes and resources. The librarian can help you ask the right questions, answer questions, look up answers, and redirect your search when you come to a dead-end.

The Internet

Without a doubt, tapping into the Internet gives you the quickest access to the most up-to-date resources available for your international job search. The Internet is valuable far beyond the specific job listings you'll find there. You can also receive career and resume assistance; take aptitude tests; subscribe to and read international publications; establish contacts; and research companies, industries, embassies, and geographical locations. You can peruse the latest edition of the *South China Morning Post* or catch the latest news in live radio broadcasts from Radio Netherlands or the Voice of Russia.

Here is where the exercises you did in Chapter 1 come in handy: The more focused you are in your quest for work abroad, the more strategic you can be when using the Internet. If you're unsure of your goals, you could spend countless hours sifting through the information you uncover on the Net, without a clear idea of its usefulness to you. If you have ever used the Internet for any reason, you know how easy it is to get side-tracked and lost for days—even weeks or months—in a sea of information once you start. Remember to keep your eyes on the prize and you'll get what you need to know in record time.

When you have identified the type of foreign employment you want, where you want to live and work abroad, and, perhaps, the name of a specific organization for which you want to work, you can start your research on the Internet. You can search according to a specific job listing, your worldwide region of choice, or a company name.

Keep in mind, however, that you won't always find every company you're interested in on the Net. And your research may lead you to conclude that only those candidates with a technical background will find international job listings. It does seem that way at present because so many of the overseas jobs listed are in the fields of high technology, finance, engineering, and health care. But a recent survey conducted by Career Mosaic, a top employment Web site, indicates that this trend may be changing as more people gain access to the Internet.

Sheer volume makes it impossible to mention all the Web sites that contain overseas job listings. And new sites crop up all the time. But a list of particularly helpful sites is included in Appendix B on page 199. Bookmark useful sites for easy reference. Use a search engine such as MetaCrawler (www.metacrawler.com) and keywords such as "international jobs," "foreign employment," and "working abroad" to find additional sites.

Colleges and Universities

You may have graduated more than a few years ago, but don't overlook your alma mater or other colleges and universities to see what career placement services and resources they might have. Services often include career counseling, access to job listings on the Internet, assistance in posting your resume on-line, and interviews with recruiters from Fortune 500 companies and smaller firms. You might have to pay a minimal fee to use these services.

Newspapers

Most job seekers are all too familiar with checking the employment ads for job listings. That's the problem. Too many prospective candidates read the same ads. Go ahead and apply if you find the perfect position—the one that has your name on it—but you'll need to distinguish yourself from the herd. Here's how:

Read the ads regularly for a sense of the marketplace and the skills and experience employers think are important. Then, expand your reading to include articles on new or growing businesses that could be a good match for your skills and expertise. Consider the hidden opportunities in companies that pique your interest. For example, when I first began my business in international training and development, I came across an article on a company that had received a grant from the U.S. Information Agency to take its show on the global road to Asia and Europe. I contacted the company, introduced myself, and soon had the opportunity to make a business presentation about my services. Reading between the lines gave me an entrée into the company. It can work for you, too, if you know what you're looking for.

Among the best newspaper resources for international employment information are the *Financial Times*, the *Wall Street Journal*, the *Asian Wall Street Journal*, and the *International Herald Tribune*. The *New York Times* and the *Los Angeles Times* can also provide leads and job listings.

Professional Associations

You are a member of at least *one* professional association, aren't you? I hope so, because membership will help you stay plugged into current trends within your industry and can provide resources for job opportunities. Many professional associations maintain a database of member resumes, sometimes for a fee, and serve as clearinghouses for employment leads. By becoming an active, visible member of your association on both the local and national level, you can maximize your chances for discovering job leads as soon as they become available.

To investigate professional trade associations in your field, look through the *Encyclopedia of Associations,* the *Encyclopedia of International Associations,* and *National Trade and Professional Associations of the United States* at your local library.

Trade Publications

What trade publications do you subscribe to or read regularly? Trade publications often list job and business opportunities in their classified ads, but you can learn about specific companies and industries and new trends and developments by reading the articles.

International Job Bulletins

Several bulletins and newsletters list international employment opportunities. Among the most popular of these publications are *Federal Career Opportunities, Federal Jobs Digest, Global Alternatives,* the *International Employment Gazette,* and the *International Employment Hotline.*

In addition, newsletters in your field of interest might occasionally list overseas job opportunities in their classified ads. How do you find these publications? Check the Internet, the local public library, your professional associations, trade publications, and career and alumni centers.

Always ask for a sample copy before subscribing to a publication, to be certain that it's of value to you. Most publishers will send at least one free issue of a publication, though usually not a current one.

Business Publications

Like trade journals, business publications can be a good source of international job listings. These publications range from local business journals to monthly magazines with a global focus. *The Economist* is perhaps the best known and most widely read source in this particular genre.

Employment Agencies and Search Firms

Employment agencies generally locate individuals for clerical and blue-collar positions. Search, or headhunter, firms find candidates for professional and technical positions. They often seek specialized experts who command high salaries.

Employment agencies generally charge applicants a fee, and few of these agencies hire for international jobs. Search firms, on the other hand, do not require a fee from applicants; they are paid by the employer, usually a percentage of the job applicant's salary.

I once attended a forum on international careers in which one of the speakers represented a local search firm. She opened her talk by stating that she was looking for an individual who was fluent in Japanese, had a Ph.D. in biochemistry, and was willing to relocate to Japan for five years. She then asked for a show of hands of audience members who fit that description. Not a soul responded, and she drove home her point, explaining how difficult it was to fill positions offered by major employers across the country.

Does that mean it's unlikely that an international headhunter can help you? Not exactly. Many search firms specialize in specific industries, such as software design, engineering, finance, insurance, health care, human resources, or sales and marketing. If one of these fields is your area of expertise, then a search firm might offer you a good international position.

Often, headhunters will find you before you find them. If you have marketed yourself professionally, you will have a much better chance of gaining the attention of the headhunters who are out there.

International Job Fairs

International School Services (ISS) sponsors three recruitment fairs annually for positions in international American schools. Apart from the academic field, however, few job fairs are devoted exclusively to recruitment for overseas positions.

Yet job fairs in general provide opportunities for large numbers of companies and prospective applicants to meet each other over a short period of time. Employers use these shows to recruit candidates for specific positions as well as to cultivate contacts with future job prospects. Prospective applicants can use job fairs to establish contacts and to learn more about the mission and values of individual companies before deciding whether or not to apply for specific openings. Typically, job fairs include helpful workshops on polishing your resume and interviewing for jobs. You will get the most value out of your time at these events if you set clear, specific goals ahead of time, determining what it is you want to accomplish by attending.

International Business Directories

Several directories list the names, addresses, and, in some cases, contact names for companies doing business overseas. One example is the *Directory of American Firms Operating in Foreign Countries*, published by World Trade Academy Press, Inc. Many directories focus on geographical regions, industries, or specific professions.

Use these directories to supplement your search resources. But do not use them to create a mailing list for blindly sending out your resume.

Outplacement Firms

Outplacement firms are geared to professionals in career transition. They provide career assessment tools, access to employment resources, and counseling on such topics as resume writing, informational and job interviews, and negotiating salary and benefits packages.

Networking Contacts

I'll spend much more time discussing networking in the next chapter, but suffice it to say that personal and professional contacts can have a profound impact on the opportunities that are offered to you throughout your lifetime. The time spent cultivating long-term business relationships is one of the most valuable investments you can make, and it will reward you a thousandfold. Keep in mind that each time you meet someone, you have the opportunity to establish a connection for future job leads abroad.

Personal Marketing

Marketing yourself means gaining visibility in your profession, so that when international job opportunities surface, those in a position to hire will think of you first. Remember the importance of letting others know what you do well and what you want to do professionally. By marketing yourself, you become a magnet, attracting international job leads rather than going after them. Believe me, it's a lot nicer, and takes far less energy in the long run, when your reputation precedes you and you start getting calls requesting your services instead of the other way around.

Headhunters often learn of prospective job candidates by reading their articles in trade journals and by listening to featured presenters at conferences. Headhunters also ask others for candidate referrals—another way your networking contacts can help you.

THE GLOBAL ENTREPRENEUR

Do you have what it takes to become a globetrotting entrepreneur? Pay attention to today's classified ads. Employers are looking for entrepreneurial types because they want decisive leaders who are self-motivated and who use critical thinking skills. The global entrepreneur must be innovative and daring, must enjoy taking risks, must know his or her business and the competition inside out, must demonstrate a solid understanding of selling and marketing at home and abroad, must manage financial resources wisely, must be able to recruit and manage diverse resources, and must do all of this while building and maintaining strategic client relationships around the world. So what do you think? Still interested in wearing the cloak of a global entrepreneur?

WHAT WILL YOU DO NEXT?

Before moving on to the next chapter, take these steps toward reaching your dream of living and working abroad. Remember to set specific, measurable, and realistic goals and a deadline for completing them. Here are a few places to start:

- Visit your local public library. Begin cultivating a working relationship with a reference librarian. Familiarize yourself with resources you can use to investigate international job opportunities. Look for information about particular companies. Conduct an Internet search.
- Enroll in a class about how to use the Internet for research.
- Select one to three professional associations for potential membership and attend meetings.
- Attend an international job fair in your area, if possible.
- Research potential search firms or outplacement firms.

3

Get Connected— Network!

If I had to name the single characteristic shared by all the truly successful people I've met in my lifetime, I'd have to say it's the ability to create and nurture a network of contacts.
—Harvey Mackay, CEO, Mackay Envelope Corporation

Some of the best resources to help you succeed in your quest for international employment are other people. In this chapter, you will learn the importance of joining professional associations and attending trade organization events. You will learn how to identify the organizations that will be the most beneficial to you and how to network with decision makers and influential people once you get involved with these organizations. In addition, you will find out how consulates, embassies, and international chambers of commerce can be important sources of information.

THE ART OF NETWORKING

Networking is a process of building personal and professional contacts with other people. Advancements in technology make it easier today than ever before to build a database of names, addresses, and phone numbers for fast contact. But successful networking—especially across cultures—involves much more than compiling a list of contacts. Networking involves developing long-term relationships with individuals at home and around the world. It involves forming connections with others through common interests, professional affiliations, association memberships, employment, industry knowledge, geographical location, friendships, and family contacts.

Mike, a demand analysis manager, explains how networking got him an international position: "I found out about my assignment in Hong Kong on a totally personal-connection basis," he says. "One of my long-time business associates in our international telecom group approached me on the q.t., asking if I knew anyone who would be interested in an international assignment for a couple of years in Hong Kong. I told him I'd like to consider it for myself."

Joe, an international business major, became friends with a Japanese colleague, Fumi, who planned to return to Japan after working in the United States. Fumi passed along Joe's name to his father, who owned a Japanese company. When Fumi went back to Japan, Joe accompanied him. Fumi's father subsequently hired Joe.

Both Mike and Joe successfully turned business connections into international job opportunities. In both cases, a personal relationship was the key. Unfortunately, we mainstream North Americans have a reputation for believing that "time is money," and we often suffer for it. We frequently come across as more interested in getting down to business than in getting to know our business associates. Yet, in many other cultures, before individuals decide whether or not they want to do business with you, they want to get to know you personally.

Networking can help take you to the next level in your international job search, but it will be of most value once you're certain what you're looking for. In my experience, people will be more than happy to help you once you tell them specifically what you want. But professional contacts can be of only limited assistance if your global search remains unfocused. Of course, you also need to know how to find the people who can best help you. We'll discuss this and more in the rest of this chapter.

If you are an experienced professional, you have an edge on beginning job seekers. After all, you've probably held at least three different positions throughout your career. You've gained hard-won experience and made countless contacts over the years. If you've traveled abroad, you've also connected with people in their countries of origin. If not, you've undoubtedly met or even hosted individuals from around the world while living in the United States. You have stayed in touch with those contacts, haven't you?

And you haven't burned any bridges, right? Well, if you're like most of us, maybe you've burned a few—but hopefully not so many that you've compromised your ability to draw on the power of your previous contacts.

Don't shortchange yourself. You probably know lots of people who can help you reach your goal of working overseas. The key is knowing how to tap into the resources you already have.

YOUR PERSONAL NETWORK

The following exercises are designed to help you identify people who can help you get work abroad. Begin by organizing your personal and professional contacts into categories. Start with those you already know—your immediate sphere of influence—and expand the list to include people you don't know, but who could be links in your international job search. Add categories as you think of them and update your list from time to time. Remember, networking is an ongoing process. Take out a sheet of paper and write down everyone you can think of in the following categories. Start with the most obvious categories first:

- People I know who are working abroad
- People I know who are living (but not working) abroad
- Former expatriates
- Frequent international business travelers
- World travelers
- Members of international organizations to which I belong
- Foreign-language teachers
- International recruiters
- International alumni
- Professors from schools that I attended
- Foreign-exchange students
- The family with whom I lived when I studied abroad

How did you do? Do you know more people in these categories than you first thought you did? If not, don't feel discouraged. Think about what you can do to start meeting people who have either traveled abroad or who come from another country. For example, you might offer to host an international visitor at work or at home. This person could be a foreign-exchange student or a member of a business or government delegation visiting your area. The National Council for Foreign Visitors makes arrangements for many such delegations through its regional councils. For more information, contact the council at 202/842-1414.

You might take a foreign-language or cooking class taught by a person from the country in which you'd like to work. Not only will you make an international contact but you'll also learn more about the culture you're hoping to join.

To expand your lists, think about people you know who might know people in the categories listed above. These contacts might include:
- Family members
- Friends
- Neighbors
- Members of your religious congregation
- Family doctors and dentists
- Family lawyer, financial planner, or accountant
- Realtor, mortgage broker, or landlord
- Teachers and day-care providers
- Professional association members
- People on your holiday card list
- Coworkers and former coworkers
- Members of your gym or social club
- Present and past clients

With these lists, you have now developed the basis for your personal network that can help you begin searching for work abroad. It's not enough to have lists of names, however. You must now reach out to those on your lists in ways that will benefit you in the long run.

HOW DO I BUILD MY NETWORK?

Networking works best when you make two things happen. First, you'll want to develop an organized system for tapping into your collection of contacts when you need them. Second, you should make a conscious and conscientious effort to stay in touch with the personal and professional contacts you have made throughout your life. It's not necessary to stay in touch often, but enough so that when you do make contact, the person will have some memory of who you are and how you know one another.

Keep notes on the person's interests, affiliations, accomplishments, likes and dislikes, and family news. Then, take advantage of opportunities to stay in touch. Here are just a few of many ideas and methods:

- Send an article that an acquaintance might enjoy or find interesting.
- Send a note telling someone that you are thinking of him or her—made even more memorable if you explain what made you think of that person.
- Notify others when you have made a change in jobs or have changed your geographic location.
- Pass along information about job or business opportunities that might be of interest to others.
- Send congratulations regarding special events or accomplishments.
- Offer a letter of introduction from one business colleague to another.
- Extend your condolences in times of misfortune.
- Express your thanks and appreciation for assistance or a gift.
- Invite another person to a special event.
- Extend a dinner invitation.
- Send a cartoon you know a colleague would enjoy.
- Send a holiday greeting.

In his popular book *The 7 Habits of Highly Effective People*, Stephen Covey discusses the importance of establishing an "emotional bank account" with another person. Most of us have bank accounts (or should have) with varying amounts of money in them. Our financial problems start when we withdraw money from those accounts without making an equal or greater amount of deposits. The results are overdrafts and bank surcharges. Covey explains that the same thing can happen in our personal and professional relationships. Too often, people initiate contact by asking for something from another person—making a withdrawal—before taking the time to invest in the relationship.

What kinds of investments might you make? Deposits such as appreciation, acceptance, loyalty, confidentiality, trust, integrity, respect, love, honor, kindness, and compassion, when made consistently and with integrity, will turn into long-term investments. You will reap the benefits of such investments many times over in the course of your life.

It's much easier to make a cash withdrawal when you have money in your account. In the same way, it's much easier to approach someone and ask for help in your job search when you have invested in the relationship ahead of time. Develop your contacts and nurture them. You never know when you may be able to help someone reach their goals or, conversely, when that person you had a brief conversation with at the gym might be able to help you reach yours. As author Deepak Chopra states, "The best way to get what you want is to help other people get what they want."

Suppose you come across the name of someone who might be able to help in your search for foreign employment but whom you don't know personally. How can you approach that person? If you received the name from a personal referral, mention that person when you make contact. If you don't have a personal referral, introduce yourself with a brief letter, stating your purpose for making contact. Explain that you will follow up with a telephone call within the week. When you do call, be very clear about what kind of help or information you are seeking. Be respectful of the person's time. Send a thank-you note after your conversation and let the person know what you did with the information you received and how it helped you.

NETWORKING THROUGH TRADE AND PROFESSIONAL ORGANIZATIONS

Trade associations and professional organizations are societies created by people of similar interests for the purpose of professional development, exchange of information, networking, and increased visibility. The organizations may be country or industry specific. Associations typically track trends in their industries and are often a good resource for job leads and referrals. Many associations have international or special-interest affiliates that could be helpful in expanding your contacts overseas. Most associations have monthly meetings, regional workshops, and annual conventions. Consequently, they are excellent places to begin building and expanding your network.

One of the best sources for information on national and international trade associations is a three-volume set titled the *Encyclopedia of Associations*, published by Gale Research. The 1999 edition lists approximately 23,000 associations in the United States, so you're bound to find at least one of interest to you. A separate volume by the same publisher, *Encyclopedia of Associations: International Organizations*, lists approximately 20,000 organizations. If you still can't find what you're looking for, check out *National Trade and Professional Associations of the United States*, which describes 7,600 trade organizations, labor unions, and technical organizations. One additional resource to consider is the *Yearbook of International Organizations*. You may have a harder time tracking this book down; none of the city libraries in my local area carried it. But if you're looking for extensive information on international organizations, this four-volume set may have just what you need.

When I ask people attending my workshops whether they belong to professional associations in their areas of interest or expertise, invariably some hands go up. Then I ask the harder question: How many of you are actively involved in these organizations? That's when most, if not all, of the hands come down. But involvement in your professional association is a critical piece of the puzzle in building a strong network. Gain visibility in your association. Volunteer to work on committees. Write articles for the association newsletter. Give a presentation at a local or national conference.

It's not always easy to begin networking at association meetings. As one workshop participant asked, "Do you know how hard it is to go up to a group of complete strangers, often men in business suits, and introduce yourself when they're six-feet tall and you're five feet, three?" I do. But it's easier to network when you've already become active in your association and know other members. Your comfort level will increase the more you practice and get involved. Volunteering to chair a committee, for example, will give you a purpose and high visibility. It will give people a chance to get to know you and to see you perform in a professional capacity.

I know it can be tough to decide which international trade associations and professional organizations to join. There are many groups, to be sure, that are only too happy to count you among their members and collect your dues. How do you choose? Here are a few guidelines for making your choice about association membership. Recognize that your time is limited, which means that you will have to select carefully. You'll probably have time for membership in only one to three associations. You want to have a life, don't you?

I recommend that you select a couple of associations and sample their meetings. You'll want to attend three different meetings to get a feel for an organization and the quality of its programming. If you attend only one meeting, one of two things will happen: Either you will love the association and sign up for membership on the spot—only to later discover that the one meeting you attended was the best one the group ever held—or you will think the meeting was so bad that you won't attend another one. But maybe the group was having an off night. By not giving them another chance, you may miss out on an association that might be a good fit for you. If you attend three meetings, you'll get a chance not only to see what's going on with a particular group but also to be seen by others.

Before signing up for membership, ask yourself these questions:
- What is the mission of the organization and does it fit with my beliefs?
- Who else belongs to this organization?
- What are the membership benefits?
- How often and where do members meet?
- Will I really attend the meetings?
- What types of events does the organization sponsor?
- Does the association have international affiliates or special global interest groups?
- Will I commit to taking an active role in the association? If so, in what capacity?
- What do I hope to gain and contribute with my membership?

The publishers of the *Encyclopedia of Associations* estimate that seven out of every ten Americans belong to at least one association. Are you one of those seven?

THE DO'S AND DON'TS OF ASSOCIATION NETWORKING

It's never a good idea to attend a meeting and immediately start passing out business cards or resumes without a good reason for doing so. Have you ever gone to a meeting and collected a lot of cards from people you didn't know only to end up throwing them in the recycling bin? That's a waste of everyone's time and money—and it's easily avoided.

The goal at meetings is not to collect as many cards as you can—it is to establish contact with those people who can be most helpful to you and whom you can help in the long run. Be selective. Rather than talk too much about yourself, start by asking questions of other people. Have a clear purpose in asking the questions. Be interested and interesting. It's OK to be ready to give a 30-second "infomercial" about yourself, but ask questions and get to know the people you're talking to first.

NETWORKING ACROSS CULTURES

If you are planning to network while traveling or living abroad, or you are a member of an international organization that puts you in contact with people from overseas, there are additional do's and don'ts of networking to keep in mind. Earlier in this chapter I mentioned the importance of taking time in building your relationships with people from other cultures. This effort is particularly important in dealing with people from Asia, Latin America, and the Middle East, where face-to-face encounters are highly valued in making and cementing personal connections.

Here are two other practices to consider. First, make a conscious effort to remember names and titles, especially in places where rank and status are revered. Second, translate your business cards into the language of your international contact and learn how to present them. Do so and you will begin to build bridges of cross-cultural understanding.

It may take longer to establish trust and develop a close working relationship with someone from abroad, but once you do, you may be treated as a member of the family and can expect business opportunities to surface quickly. Reciprocity and mutual respect are the cornerstones of networking internationally.

FOREIGN CONSULATES AND EMBASSIES

The United States operates more than 250 diplomatic and consular posts around the world. Their mission is to protect the interests of American citizens who are traveling, living, and working abroad. In 1997, for instance,

U.S. consular offices responded to approximately 14,000 requests for assistance by private citizens abroad. Such assistance included medical care, evacuation, the adoption of children, and the replacement of lost or stolen passports. In the same way, foreign consulates operating in the United States provide assistance to their citizens in this country.

Although their primary purpose is to help their own citizens, foreign consulates in the United States can also answer inquiries related to immigration, visas, work permits, tourism, business, trade organizations, and housing in their countries for American citizens who are planning to travel abroad. Therefore, foreign consulates can be another valuable resource for you in planning to live and work abroad.

Embassies are representatives of their governments abroad, and their mission is diplomacy. Like foreign consulates, embassies can also be valuable sources of information for U.S. citizens planning to go abroad. All foreign embassies in the United States are located in Washington, D.C., with only one embassy per country (consulates maintain regional offices).

For more information, contact the U.S. State Department and request copies of *The Diplomatic List*, a publication listing all the foreign embassies in the United States, and *Foreign Consular Offices in the United States*. You can also find this information on the Internet at the U.S. State Department's Web site: http://travel.state.gov.

INTERNATIONAL CHAMBERS OF COMMERCE

You may already be a member of your local chamber of commerce. If you are, then you know that this organization provides comprehensive information in a variety of areas to help local businesses. Chambers host forums for exchanging information, educational workshops, and networking events for their members. Like regional and national associations, chambers of commerce can also provide leads for overseas employment opportunities.

International chambers of commerce take the mission of local chambers one step further by helping companies expand their markets and connect their products and services with customers around the world. By contacting international chambers of commerce with offices in the United States, you can gather critical business and country information before venturing abroad. You can also contact American Chambers of Commerce Abroad, which are associations of American companies doing business in particular countries.

International and American chambers of commerce offer news bulletins and briefings on market conditions and business environments in host countries; trade leads; business and government contact information; and information on custom duties, tariffs, and regulations. For more information on international chambers of commerce, check http://worldchambers.net.

WHAT WILL YOU DO NEXT?

Before continuing on to the next chapter, take the following steps toward your dream of living and working abroad. Remember to set specific, measurable, and realistic goals and a deadline for completing them. Here are a few places to start:

- Complete your list of networking contacts.
- Decide who you will call and with what goals in mind.
- Decide who you will meet with and with what goals in mind.
- Reestablish contact with at least five members of your personal network.
- Decide which international trade associations you wish to join and become active in.
- Contact an embassy, consulate, or international chamber of commerce for information on living and doing business abroad.

4

Get Support—Ask!

I was fortunate to have a teacher who convinced me that the idea of becoming an Egyptologist was not silly but sensible and eminently possible if I seriously worked at it.
        —Kent R. Weeks, discoverer of the lost tomb KV5

It's a myth to think that somehow you must come up with all the answers yourself when seeking international employment. Sometimes the easiest means of getting what you want is simply to ask for help.

In this chapter you will discover how to continue building long-term, mutually beneficial relationships. You'll learn how to associate with those who believe in you and have the skills and expertise to help you achieve your dream of working abroad. You will learn how to approach informational interviews, follow up on leads and referrals, and create support groups to keep you on track as you move toward your goal of working overseas.

ROLE MODELS AND MENTOR RELATIONSHIPS

Here's where your networking pays off. By now you've probably met some pretty amazing people who might be doing exactly what you want to do. Perhaps it is a person who leads river tours up the Amazon. Maybe it is a foreign correspondent you saw speaking at a local lecture or an expatriate returning from a Peace Corps assignment in Guatemala. You might have spoken with a globetrotting executive or entrepreneur for a telecommunications company in Singapore. Any one of these individuals can be an effective role model for you because she or he has made it abroad. By analyzing how these people made it overseas, you can learn what to do to follow in their footsteps.

If you make only brief contact with someone you view as a role model, you may not learn anything. The benefit to you ends with your brief encounter. A mentoring relationship, on the other hand, takes the concept of role model a step further. Here you establish a definite association with an experienced and trusted advisor who can guide you in your efforts to find work abroad. Mentoring goes well beyond answering a few questions and directing you to others. A mentor takes a personal, vested interest in helping you succeed.

HOW CAN A MENTOR HELP ME?

If you're a seasoned professional, you already know how valuable role models and mentors are to your success. Now let's put the mentoring idea into the context of international employment. When you're seeking work abroad, an effective mentor can be of enormous help in several significant ways. First, a mentor can recommend an overall global career or business strategy for you. A mentor can also help in building relationships.

Marshall is an international sales manager based in Singapore. He credits his mentor with helping him step around the political, social, and cultural land mines associated with working in Asia. By following the lead of his mentor, Marshall learned to take time in building his relationships with the Japanese. As Marshall describes it: "From observing my mentor in action, I learned not to brag and how to be a gentleman in the Japanese culture. I also learned that in Asia, business is done on the basis of a handshake [and] whom you know and face-to-face."

Marshall toned down the aggressiveness that had gotten him his overseas position in the first place and became a more effective listener. His patience and willingness to adapt to the norms of Japanese business won him a loyal client following. As a result of his mentor's guidance, he avoided many of the missteps that could have sabotaged his success overseas. Mentors can also introduce you to members of their own international network or help you connect with people who might not talk to you otherwise. Sometimes a satisfied client can play this role. Once I had tried unsuccessfully to set up an informational interview with the director of an educational institution. Several months later, one of my regular clients suggested I contact the same person, not knowing that I'd already made the attempt. Acting on her advice, I contacted the educational director again. This time, I got the results I wanted, all because I used my client's name as my calling card.

Additionally, your mentor can let you know about hot leads for an international assignment. Mentors can even put in a plug for you with an international recruiter. Once you're offered an international position, your mentor can help you negotiate a contract. He or she can also give advice on managing the experience of living abroad for yourself and your family. Good mentors can give you insider tips about the best and worst of their experiences and can help you overcome obstacles. In a nutshell, a good mentor can help you get where you want to go more easily and more quickly than, in all likelihood, you could do on your own.

WHAT DO I NEED TO ASK FIRST?

As you reflect on the people you've met through networking, consider which ones would be a good fit for you as mentors. When approaching a potential mentor, discuss these questions together before making a final decision:

- Has the person "been there and done that"? Was he or she successful in doing what you want to do? You'll learn more from someone who has succeeded than from someone who is willing to share only what didn't work.
- Is the person accessible and willing and able to invest time and energy in your relationship? Unless the person can make a commitment to spend time with you, it doesn't much matter how successful he or she has been in getting work abroad.
- What do you want and expect from the mentoring relationship? What does the potential mentor expect from you in return? Are you willing and able to give it? Are your expectations compatible? Be clear about your expectations and goals up front so that you can avoid misunderstandings later on.

- How often will you get together and by what means? Do you want to meet only occasionally or at regularly set times? Maybe you can't meet with your mentor in person because of geographical distance. If so, it's important to establish a nurturing relationship through regular contact by phone or by e-mail.

WHAT DOES MY MENTOR GET FROM THE RELATIONSHIP?

Remember that the mentoring relationship is a two-way street. Your mentor won't agree to help you unless the association promises to be beneficial to him or her as well. For some people, the intrinsic satisfaction of helping another person benefit from their experiences will be enough motivation. Others are simply flattered to be asked for help. By asking successful expatriates for their assistance, you give them a chance to tell their stories to an interested audience. In general, people love to talk about their experiences working abroad and will go out of their way to help you succeed.

One way to develop credibility with your mentor is to follow up on his or her suggestions—to take the person's advice seriously and to actually do something with it. You can also express appreciation for your mentor's assistance by introducing him or her to people in your network and passing along referrals and job leads. As you develop your relationship and get to know your mentor better, you will undoubtedly think of other ways in which you can reciprocate his or her assistance.

Sometimes your mentor might be the one who initiates the relationship. Sometimes you might be the initiator. In either case, it's up to you to follow through and keep your mentor informed of your progress. He or she will want to know about your continuing challenges and successes in getting work abroad.

WHAT ABOUT INTERNATIONAL JOB COUNSELORS?

If you're still in school or recently graduated, you may be able to find an international job counselor at your alma mater. Outside of academia, you'll find career-counseling services listed in the yellow pages. Executive recruiters will sometimes offer job-counseling services, and outplacement firms certainly do.

Keep in mind, though, that you have to find job counselors who are familiar with *international* job search strategies. That's not an easy thing to do. Unless they're specialists, most job counselors don't realize the differences between applying for work at home and applying for jobs overseas—and there are significant differences. Unwittingly, job counselors using conventional job-hunting skills may steer global job seekers in the wrong direction.

So-called international job counselors, especially in small or understaffed career centers, may be that in name only. Most likely, they've had the mantle bestowed upon them without any credentials specific to the international job market. Still, even with limited resources, a job counselor should be able to help you make important links and conduct research on the Internet.

The most effective job counseling for international assignments is holistic in approach. It should take several factors into consideration: your motivation, personal attributes, career goals, desires, skills, and credentials; the current outlook for jobs abroad in terms of both region and industry; and international hiring practices. Effective international job counselors have either worked abroad themselves or have developed a specialty in this area through personal interest or contacts. They know what resources are available to help you locate the work you want overseas and how to get you quickly plugged into the global marketplace.

Before investing either your time or money in a career service, however, ask yourself a few questions:

- What's my goal in meeting with a job specialist?
- What do I hope and expect to gain?
- Are there alternatives to the job counselor's services?
- How much time and money am I willing to invest in this process?
- How will I measure the success of our meetings?

Then ask the international job counselor a few questions:

- What percentage of your counseling work is spent dealing with the international job market?
- What are your credentials, background, and experience in the global job market?

- What can you do to help me find work abroad?
- What tools, techniques, and assessments do you use?
- Can you tell me some success stories about applicants who found work abroad after meeting with you?
- Can I contact three people who have used your services?
- What will your services cost?

Skilled international job-counseling services are few and far between. If you're unable to locate such advisors, your best bet is to conduct the necessary research yourself. You've already taken an important step in that direction by reading this book.

SUCCESS SUPPORT GROUPS FOR GOING GLOBAL

Remember the expression "Two heads are better than one"? That's certainly true when it comes to searching for work overseas. In his famous book, *Think and Grow Rich,* Napoleon Hill introduces the concept of "the Master Mind." He describes it as "coordination of knowledge and effort, in a spirit of harmony, between two or more people, for the attainment of a definite purpose."

The Master Mind principle explains that when you surround yourself with people who are intelligent and experienced and have your best interests at heart, amazing things can happen. In the same way, when you create a "success support group" for going global, you can reach your goals faster—by capitalizing on the research, experience, and insights of others. At the same time, you can help contribute to the future success of those in your group by sharing helpful information and referrals.

How does this system work exactly? While there are no fixed rules for formulating your own Master Mind group, there are a few steps you can take to create a group and to maximize its effectiveness. The most essential step is to select the members of your group with great care. Most importantly, find people who will do what they say they're going to do— everything from attending scheduled meetings to following up on other members' advice and suggestions to reporting back at the next meeting. You'll want to find other group members who are at least at your professional level, however you define that. Ideally, some members should be a notch above you in terms of background and experience.

Limit the number of participants to a manageable size—usually between six and eight people. If you decide to go with a lower number, each member must be willing to assume greater responsibility—with a commitment to show up for meetings and to both solicit help and give it. If you go with a larger number of members, you'll have less reason to worry if one or more people can't make it to a particular meeting. You'll also have the benefit of more people who can offer one another assistance. The drawback, of course, is that larger groups can become unwieldy, and you may not have ample opportunity to involve each person at each meeting.

A Master Mind group for going global can offer much of the same support as a mentor can. In both cases, you'll benefit from other people's experience. You can discover strategies about what to do and what not to do when seeking work abroad that can shave weeks—even months—off your learning curve. When the group begins to see the positive results that come from sharing information and developing strategies together, everyone becomes energized to do more and to succeed even faster. It's exciting to see people achieve their dreams.

THE INFORMATIONAL INTERVIEW

An informational interview is just that. It's an informational meeting with someone who might be able to help in your global job search. During the informational interview, you're looking for suggestions and advice, not a job or assignment. You won't do yourself any favors if you use the pretext of an informational interview to make a pitch for a job instead. Besides, if you leapfrog right to the job interview, you'll miss out on a treasure trove of information.

The right informational interview can help you discover how your contact person developed his or her global career path, which may give you some ideas of your own. You might also learn about the following:
- Specific international positions
- What it's like to live and work abroad on your own or with family members

- Trends in hiring for short-term and long-term positions abroad
- How to get the kind of international assignment you want
- What credentials you'll need for an overseas assignment
- How you can bolster your resume and credentials so that you stand out in a crowd of applicants
- Salary ranges for the position you want
- Managing your relocation overseas
- What to expect once your international assignment is finished
- Referrals to other people who could be helpful contacts

Eureka! A well-thought-out informational interview can save you countless hours of research. But be sure to use the informational interview in conjunction with, not instead of, other research. To get the most benefit from an informational interview, you'll want to take the following steps:

Before Requesting Your Interview

As anyone who's ever tackled a house remodeling project will tell you, preparation is *everything*. The same is true with the informational interview. Here are three ways to set yourself up for a successful outcome:

Research Do as much research before requesting an informational interview as possible. You'll create a favorable impression and maximize your time if you do. You won't be wasting the other person's time—and hurting your credibility—by asking questions you could easily have found answers to elsewhere. Find out as much as possible about the person you want to interview and the organization for which he or she works. Ask whoever referred you for guidance here.

A colleague who specializes in global communication services once complained to me about unsolicited phone calls. Usually, these calls came from individuals wanting to know how to break into her field. Too often, she was besieged by questions from people who weren't respectful of her time and had only the vaguest idea of how she could help them. Don't repeat their mistakes. If you're not clear about what you want from the people you hope to interview, everybody loses—including you.

Prepare Specific Questions The clearer you are in your goals for working abroad, the easier it will be to formulate your interview questions. Think about the type of position you want, the type of organization for which you want to work, and the place you want to live. Use this information as a frame of reference in preparing your questions.

Preparing your questions ahead of time doesn't necessarily mean that you'll ask all of them, but it will help you direct the course of the interview to ensure that you'll end up getting the information you want. Preparation will allow you to be more spontaneous in your follow-up questions, without losing sight of your overall objective.

Polish Your CV or Resume You'll want to bring a copy of your resume or CV to the informational interview. The contact person might want to review it afterward at his or her convenience. The resume will also give the person an easy way to get in touch with you if international job opportunities arise after the interview. Of course, if you plan to ask for advice about your resume during the informational interview, you'll need to bring it with you. (In the next chapter, I cover the specifics of preparing international resumes, CVs, and cover letters.)

Requesting an Informational Interview

Now that you know what kind of information you want, it's time to contact the person you wish to interview. You have several options in this regard. You could make a telephone call or send an e-mail or fax to request an appointment.

It's sometimes difficult to get past a company's gatekeepers, though. Unless you have a personal referral, be prepared to get no response. Many people view unsolicited e-mail messages as spamming and automatically delete them without reading them. The same holds true for unsolicited faxes. They're often thrown out before ever reaching their intended recipients.

The most courteous approach when requesting an informational interview is to write a brief, sincere letter. In the letter, you should identify yourself, mention the person who referred you (if applicable), explain your purpose in making contact, explain how you think the recipient can help you, and mention your intent to follow up with a phone call to schedule an interview (naturally, at the other person's convenience).

Avoid asking specific questions in your letter, since you will be asking these questions in person during the interview.

You're more likely to be granted an informational interview if you ask for a brief (10- to 15-minute) telephone conversation or meeting. Most people are willing to give you 15 minutes of their time, especially when someone they know has referred you. Any more than 15 minutes might start to feel intrusive—most people are rather protective of their time.

You might think that this time limit is unrealistic. How could you possibly gain any significant information in 15 minutes? Is it really worth your energy to meet with someone for that short a time? In truth, the interview might last longer. But when you ask for 15 minutes, you're more likely to receive an informational interview than if you ask for, say, 30 minutes. Chances are, if the interview is going well, the person will ignore the 15-minute limit and continue the interview.

Remember, if you invite someone to an informational interview over lunch, you're expected to foot the bill. But I don't recommend this approach—your international job search shouldn't have to cost much money. In addition, the people you'll be interviewing probably haven't met you before. They might be reluctant to give you an hour of their time right off the bat, even for a great lunch.

Even if my colleague in global communication services wanted to, she simply doesn't have the time to talk to everyone who asks for an informational interview. She has to deny most requests. You can often overcome similar resistance by being brief, getting right to the point about what you want, and mentioning the name of a person who referred you.

Lights! Camera! Action! The Interview Itself

While the informational interview is typically less formal and structured than a job interview, your goal is still to create a positive impression. First impressions count—from the clothing you wear to the way you shake hands to the tone and energy of your voice (especially during a phone interview) to the confidence of your walk and your overall demeanor. You want the people you interview to remember you as someone they'd be happy to recommend for a bona fide job.

How exactly do you want to be remembered after you walk out the door or hang up the telephone? What three to five words or phrases capture the impression you want to make? Once you've figured that out, decide what you can do to create that impression. Let's say you want to come across as someone who's confident and self-assured. What could you say or do to communicate this image?

A confident person walks fast—but not too fast—with head up, eyes focused directly ahead, and shoulders back. In mainstream North American culture, a confident person has a firm—but not too strong—handshake that resonates with both men and women. If you're interviewing someone from a different cultural background or someone from a foreign-owned company, be sure you do your homework about that person's culture and culturally appropriate behavior. Think carefully about the impression you want to create and consider what you can do to ensure that your goal is met.

Extend Culturally Appropriate Greetings The amount of time spent on initial greetings and small talk will vary, according to whom you're speaking with and where. In mainstream North America, it's important to get down to business because "time is money." Therefore, here at home you should generally spend minimal time on the preliminaries. However, if you're speaking with someone in Asia, Mexico, or the Middle East, you can expect the time spent on preliminary greetings to be considerably longer. Your host may want to know your impressions of his or her country, about your family, about your trip if you have just arrived, and other such matters. Let your host set the stage in this regard. You certainly don't want to rush into your questions without taking the time to build your relationship with someone who can help you.

Get Down to Business Following your initial greeting and introductions, begin by mentioning the name of the person who referred you, if there was one, and reiterate your purpose in conducting the informational interview. State your international job goal clearly and explain how you think the person you're interviewing can be of most assistance.

Here's a sample opener: "Thanks for taking the time to see me today, Ms. Donahue. Peter Mack thought you would be a good person for me to speak to. He said you'd been a PR director for an environmental services firm in Jakarta recently. I'm exploring job assignments in the same field in Asia. I'm wondering if you could offer me advice on how I might follow in your footsteps."

Ask Effective Questions   With a 15-minute time frame, consider what information you want to gather in that short period. You've already prepared the questions you want to ask; have two or three of the most important questions at hand as you begin your interview.

To produce quality results, your questions need to be clear, purposeful, and focused. This means that everyone must understand the questions— there should be no ambiguity in what you're asking. If the meaning or intent of your question is confusing, then it's a good bet that the answer you receive will be equally confusing.

You should also have a good reason for asking a particular question. When you know where you're headed with a question—what you're trying to learn—you'll be better able to assess the response you receive. Then you can continue with a follow-up question that will provide you with an even greater depth of information.

If you're seeking an international assignment exactly like the one held by the person you're interviewing, you can ask open-ended questions related to the person's job experience. Here are a few examples:
- What were your job title and responsibilities overseas?
- How did you get your international assignment?
- What was a typical workday like for you?
- What was it like to live and work in Jakarta [or another location]?
- What do you wish you'd known before accepting your international assignment?
- What did you enjoy the most and least about your time spent working abroad?
- How was your experience similar to and different from what you expected?
- What were your credentials and work experience prior to accepting the assignment?
- What was your experience like in returning home?

Now you can start to talk about yourself. Link the answers you receive to questions about your own situation. For example:

- What do you think the current demand is in Asia for people in this field?
- What kind of salary range can I expect?
- Based on your experience, how would you suggest I approach XYZ Company?
- What do you see as the strengths of my resume and what areas would you suggest I improve?
- What would you suggest I do to strengthen my odds of getting work abroad?

Be prepared to explain what you've already done up to this point in your job search. If you've run into problems or obstacles in getting the information you need, ask the person for suggestions about solutions. Whatever you do, don't request a list of companies you should contact. Finding those companies is your work, remember? If you have a specific question about a particular organization, that's a different story.

Listen Attentively Have you ever watched a television journalist ask a question, get a response, then proceed with another question that's totally unrelated to what the speaker said? Aren't you frustrated on those occasions, wishing the interviewer would follow up on the first answer?

Don't let this happen to you when you're conducting an informational interview. Be interesting and *interested* throughout. After you ask questions, be sure to listen attentively to the responses you get, then follow up with related questions. Don't become so focused on your own words that you fail to hear valuable, unexpected information from the other person. Periodically check in with yourself and ask: Am I listening—or am I just waiting to talk?

Wrap Up the Interview As you near the end of your interview, conclude with questions such as:
- Given what you know now about your international job experience, would you do it again? Why or why not?
- Are there any questions that I haven't asked that you think I should have?
- Are there other individuals in the field who you recommend that I speak to? If so, who?

- May I leave my resume with you in the event that you hear of an international job opportunity in this field?

Honor Your Time Commitment   Remember your promise to take only 15 minutes of the other person's time. Bring it to the person's attention by saying something like, "I'm enjoying our conversation, and your insights are invaluable to me. But I did promise to keep our interview to 15 minutes, and I see our time is up." If the other person wants to either end the interview or continue talking, this is his or her cue to let you know, one way or the other. He or she might suggest continuing the discussion at a later date. At the end of the interview, of course, be certain to thank the person for his or her time.

After the Interview

An important element of etiquette that's often overlooked after an informational interview is the thank-you letter. You can stand out in a crowd simply by taking a few moments to write to the person you interviewed. A handwritten note is more personal and thoughtful than a typed letter. Be sure, of course, that your handwriting is legible.

A good thank-you letter should be brief, written on personal stationery if you have it, and sent within 48 hours. Thank the person you interviewed for his or her time and information and mention any advice you found particularly helpful, as well as what you plan to do with the advice.

Take Action   Sift through the information you took away from your interview. Plan a course of action based on the advice you received or any ideas that came to you via the interview. Unless you act on the information you received, you've simply had a pleasant conversation. That's nice, but it won't lead you any closer to your goal of working abroad.

Keep Your Contacts Informed   Stay in touch with people you interview and let them know whether or not you were successful in following their advice. Most people you interview will want to know how you're progressing toward your goal of working abroad. They are now part of your ever-expanding personal network, and it's up to you to find reasons and ways to stay in touch. You should also check back with the person who recommended a particular interview in the first place. Tell him or her how the interview went and what you got out of it.

Follow Up on Leads If you've generated leads and referrals through your networking and informational interviews, follow up on them. Surprisingly, follow-through is where most people lose out. They have no problems asking for what they want, but they neglect to follow up on the valuable information they receive.

If, in the course of an informational interview, you learn that you should revise your CV, do so at your earliest opportunity. You don't gain anything by waiting. If you're told to get in touch with a particular person, do so—and be certain to use the name of the person who referred you. You'll want to build momentum that will take you to your goal.

Create a system for managing the names, addresses, and phone numbers of people in your personal network as it continues to grow. Keep track of the information you get, act on it, then check items off your list of things to do. Keep weeding and cultivating your contacts, just like you do the plants in your garden.

WHAT WILL YOU DO NEXT?

Before you continue to the next chapter, take these steps toward your dream of living and working abroad. Remember to set specific, measurable, and realistic goals and deadlines for completing them.

- Make a list of your role models and mentors in the international field.
- Ask targeted individuals for mentoring relationships.
- Research three to five companies or individuals in preparation for informational interviews.
- Contact three to five people to request informational interviews.
- Finalize questions for informational interviews.
- Establish a system for organizing your leads and referrals.
- Set up a success support group for going global.

5

Get It Together— Prepare!

Adventure is something you seek for pleasure, or even for profit, like a gold rush or invading a country . . . but experience is what really happens to you in the long run; the truth that finally overtakes you.

—Katherine Anne Porter, writer

By now you know what it is you want and what you have to do to get it. This chapter shows you how to put your promotional materials together and how to market yourself for international employment. You'll receive tips for preparing a cover letter, curriculum vitae (CV), and resume and for developing a "success portfolio." You will also find advice on how to fill in the gaps when you're short on the required skills and experience.

PREPARING YOUR APPLICATION MATERIALS

Remember, your goal is to get hired by an international employer. Regardless of where you're applying, here are a few general tips to keep in mind:

Tailor Your Materials

It's OK to prepare a general resume to give to friends and other contacts who can refer you to potential international positions. However, when applying for specific positions, you'll want to personalize each cover letter and resume.

And be sure to send the cover letter, international resume or CV, and support material *as requested* by the potential employer or the international job announcement. Note that I emphasize "as requested." You should send nothing more, nothing less than that which is requested. If you don't include everything that's requested, you could be eliminated from the hiring process on that basis alone. If you send more than requested, there's a good chance the materials will end up in the wastebasket.

When I served as director of an international organization, occasionally I'd receive extensive packets of information from job applicants. While I didn't throw the extraneous information away, I didn't read it either. Instead, I filed the information away and never looked at it again.

Create a Professional Image

To present a professional image, always use quality correspondence materials and proofread your writing meticulously. International employers do not expect to see typos, and you could easily be eliminated from stiff competition because of them. Jack, an American recruiter based in Qatar, elaborates: "When someone is looking at a pile of 50 to 100 resumes for a position, the ones that contain grammatical errors or poor sentence structure will be the first to be eliminated."

Ask another person to read over your application materials, since it's easy to overlook typos and other errors. If you insist on doing the proofreading yourself, consider this common suggestion: Start at the end of your work and read backward. That way, you won't be distracted by content, only the errors. Personally, this technique makes me nauseated, but if it works for you, go for it!

Do Your Homework

Take the initiative to find out the name of your potential employer, as well as his or her title, and address your correspondence accordingly. If you got the person's name from a directory, take the time to verify it. With the high level of turnover in organizations today, the name in the directory could very likely be wrong.

It's more challenging to get the name of a person when applying for a position overseas, of course. Yet using the right name and title will get you further ahead in the application process. As a last resort, refer to the person by title, with a salutation such as "Dear International Marketing

Director." Be particularly careful to find out if the person is male or female, however. You won't score any points with female employers by beginning your letter "Dear Sir."

Once you know who will be receiving your application, you'll have some decisions to make. You'll need to decide which resume format to use and which skills and work experiences to highlight. Keep in mind that what one employer finds essential on a resume may be irrelevant to another. A foreign-owned organization, for instance, may be just as interested in your extracurricular activities as in your work experience.

Note that it's a courtesy—if not a necessity—to attach a translation of your resume to the original. This practice will help build a respectful relationship with your reader. Yet translating the specifics of your work history and education into a foreign language will be a challenge. If you're not totally fluent in the language, it's best to hire a professional translator.

WHAT ABOUT COVER LETTERS?

Apart from the envelope (if your application arrives by mail), your cover letter is the first chance you have to make a positive impression on a potential employer. The letter should be brief but informative. It should be no more than one page in length and should typically contain three paragraphs.

In the first paragraph, state the position for which you're applying and how you learned about the international job opportunity. If you're applying to an American employer, it's best to use a dynamic opening that captures the reader's attention immediately. Elaborate on the benefits you will bring to the advertised position.

Use the second paragraph to give a brief synopsis of your background, experience, and personal attributes—specifically those that fit the requirements and qualifications mentioned in the job announcement. If you're not responding to a particular job announcement, focus on the mission and values of the organization to which you're applying. You've done your homework on this, right? Make the link between what you've learned about the organization and your personal and professional characteristics. Explain why you and the organization would be a good fit. Emphasize the results of your past accomplishments.

In the final paragraph, state confidence in your ability to contribute to the success of the organization. Close with an action step—what you will do next. Indicate the best times for the employer to reach you, so that you can minimize the game of "phone tag."

Tailoring Your Cover Letter

Your cover letter should be culturally appropriate for your intended reader. For instance, in mainstream North America, it's perfectly appropriate, even expected, for job candidates to push their credentials forward—both in cover letters and during job interviews. If you're applying to a Japanese company, however, this strategy is likely to backfire. To impress a Japanese employer, it's more appropriate to emphasize your contributions to the team's success than your own individual achievements. As the Japanese aphorism goes, "The nail that sticks up gets hammered down." And since business in Japan is conducted on the basis of whom you know, it's virtually a waste of time to send a cover letter and resume without a personal referral.

Handwritten Letters

When applying to European employers, you may be asked to handwrite the cover letter that accompanies your international resume or CV. Many European companies hire experts who then assess applicants' personal attributes on the basis of their handwriting. If your handwriting is almost indecipherable, this might be a good time to make some adjustments!

European employers may use the information from your handwriting analysis in a couple of different ways. In some cases, they may use it to weed out undesirable applicants. In others, the analysis becomes a tool for discussion with the candidate, either during the job interview or after hiring.

INTERNATIONAL CVs AND RESUMES

If you're applying for an overseas position with an American employer, your resume should be the same as one you would use when applying for a domestic position. Foreign employers, however, generally seek more in-depth personal data from applicants than do American employers. Many foreign companies place great importance on the character and social

FILLING IN THE GAPS

If you prepare your resume, CV, or success portfolio and notice gaps in your skills or experience, here are several steps you can take to remedy the situation:

Take Classes: If you lack some important skills, technical or otherwise, consider enrolling in a class at a local college or university. It's a relatively painless way to get up to speed on desirable work skills. One class may be sufficient, or you may wish to enroll in a longer certificate or advanced degree program.

Be certain that taking such a step will make a difference in your employment chances before making the investment, however. Ask the program director if the school tracks the placement of its graduates. Ask for names of recent graduates who have gotten positions because of the advanced degree or certificate program you're considering. You might ask to speak with alumni about their experiences in the program. Consider different schools, comparing cost, content, and placement before making your decision.

Do Volunteer Work: International volunteer work is another way to fill in the gaps of your global work experience. Many before you have taken the plunge and volunteered for such organizations as the Peace Corps, CARE, and Amnesty International. Those who have certainly did not do so for the money. Overseas volunteers attest to the intrinsic satisfaction of working where their job skills are desperately needed and greatly appreciated. In many cases, even if no salary is available, volunteers receive a small stipend, along with a housing and food allowance. In some cases, volunteer organizations pay relocation costs.

Apply for an Internship: Internships offer an excellent way to make valuable contacts and add to your personal network database. They provide opportunities for you to practice what you've learned in the classroom and to develop critical work skills. They also give you a chance to experience working in a particular kind of organization or place. Internships benefit the employer by filling a staffing void and bringing a fresh perspective to the organization.

Internships come in several varieties: paid, unpaid, with a small stipend, or for academic credit. They are offered through educational institutions, the government, private companies, and nonprofit organizations and may or may not take place abroad. In most cases, interns gain a wealth of hands-on work experience in a short time—usually six months to a year.

Investigate a number of internship programs before pursuing one. While many internships are geared specifically to college students or recent graduates, opportunities also exist for working people and those reentering the workforce. If you don't find quite what you're looking for, get creative and design your own internship. Think about the kind of company or organization for which you'd like to work and think about why. Then develop a strategy for approaching key people in such organizations with an internship proposal.

If you're lucky, you might land an international internship. The value of such a position goes far beyond network building and gaining real-world job experience. When based abroad, you can see what it's like to live and work in a foreign country. If you do accept an overseas internship, your employer should complete the paperwork for your stay in the host country. It's in your best interests to keep on top of the process, however, because the wheels of government paperwork can grind slowly.

Finally, internships provide a safety net—knowing that the assignment lasts for only a short period. If the job is not what you're looking for, you haven't invested so much that you'll regret the experience.

standing of job applicants. They want to learn more about you than just your professional accomplishments.

The Traditional CV

Often, an international organization may request a CV as part of your job application. CV stands for "curriculum vitae," which, loosely translated from Latin, means "life story." The employer requesting a CV expects a person's life story to be longer than one or two pages. In fact, CVs are traditionally five to eight pages long.

Unlike a resume, a CV should include several pages of personal information, such as your country of citizenship, gender, age, marital status, family members and their occupations, religious affiliation, health, hobbies, and interests. The CV should also include your photograph.

You're probably not used to divulging such personal information to strangers and potential colleagues. You might not like the idea at all. After all, it's discriminatory and illegal in the United States for an employer to ask about your age, ethnic background, marital status, family members, or sexual orientation. The same antidiscrimination laws that apply at home protect you when you work for a U.S. employer overseas. But foreign employers operate under different laws, and the request for personal information is allowed.

You might worry when you include your photograph with your application that you will run the risk of being rejected because of it. In fact, you might—though not necessarily for the reasons you might think. Walid, a business instructor from the Middle East, describes the importance of seeing a job applicant's photograph: "Our culture is based on reading the energy from your face. It's an intuitive way of knowing your substance. Gender and age is not the issue." Ultimately, you'll have to decide for yourself how much personal information you feel comfortable including on your international resume.

Changing Trends

In the past, the short resume format just didn't cut it with many foreign employers because of their desire for detailed applicant information. But times are changing, and these changes are driven in part by the fast pace of our global marketplace. Francoise, a former recruiter for a French manufacturing company, explains: "We must read it in a few minutes, because now we receive a lot of CVs each day."

Indeed, many foreign employers now favor the one- to two-page international resume over the traditional five- to eight-page CV. In fact, when referring to the shorter format, the terms "international resume" and "CV" are often used interchangeably. In both cases, the personal data is often compressed into one paragraph instead of several pages. Japanese employers have actually made resume writing easy for job applicants by creating a standardized two-page resume format. The forms are available for sale in Japanese stationery stores.

What to Include

When preparing your resume for work in the United States, you've probably used the reverse chronological format—listing your most recent work experience first. Be aware that in some countries, such as Japan, the opposite is expected. You're supposed to list your work experience in chronological order, starting with your first professional job.

In addition to the names of organizations for which you have worked, dates of employment, and company locations, international (and American) employers will want to know your job titles, specific responsibilities, and accomplishments on the job. Be detailed in providing this information and avoid using acronyms or abbreviations that foreign employers may find unfamiliar.

Increasingly, international companies want employees who have taken on progressively greater levels of responsibility in business and people management. Management skills indicate a grasp of interpersonal relations and the ability to communicate and make decisions—all essential attributes when working abroad. International employers also value evidence of initiative and technical competence.

Like domestic companies, international employers will want to know about your educational background. If you're applying for work in a particularly status-driven country, such as Japan, the more prestigious the schools you've attended the better.

Don't forget to include your extracurricular and volunteer activities on your international resume. Also note any special recognition, honors, or certificates you've received.

Highlight Your International Experience

Savvy international employers know that working abroad is not for every-one. Even if you've been successful in positions in the United States, that doesn't mean that you're guaranteed to succeed outside the country.

Employers have a lot riding on your success, not the least of which is the financial investment they'll have to make in relocating you and your family overseas. Therefore, be certain that your resume includes any information that demonstrates your adaptability to living and working overseas. Perhaps you've traveled or worked internationally in the past. If you've done so for extended periods, so much the better. Mention programs of foreign-language study, second-language fluency, and your participation in a foreign-exchange program or internship. Even if this experience isn't recent history, it indicates that you know what it means to live and work in an international environment.

Don't Forget the Basics

Whether you're writing a CV or a resume, some items are standard. For one thing, employers need to know how to get in touch with you. They need to know your name and address, telephone number, and, if you really want to be accessible, your fax number and e-mail address.

Include your job objective on your international resume, even if you've already mentioned it in your cover letter. Indeed, you can't assume that the cover letter and resume will necessarily stay together. They might be passed around to various team interviewers, and pages can get lost.

CREATING A SUCCESS PORTFOLIO

We often think of artists and architects as the only people with portfolios. Yet anyone seeking work abroad should create a "success portfolio." Consider it an extensive promotional packet. Include such items as a professional black-and-white photograph of yourself, candid photos of yourself in action at work, your business card, a resume, work project summaries, testimonials or letters of recommendation, a client list, certificates from continuing education programs, and a summary of personal and professional accomplishments.

The portfolio will serve several purposes. First, it is an easy way to organize any information that a potential employer might request. Everything will be easily accessible at a moment's notice. Second, the portfolio will be a visual reminder of how much you've done in your career. This reminder can help you stay motivated when business prospects are not as abundant as you'd like. Third, the portfolio will help you see at a glance what essentials might be missing in your background. It will give you an impetus to go out and get the missing experience.

When you create your own success portfolio, you will get most of the benefits. It's unlikely that you will ever show everything in the portfolio to a prospective employer, but you'll have it ready just in case.

Think about what you'll want to include in your own success portfolio. Remember to focus on your international background, which can make you more desirable to employers abroad. This is a fun and creative project, so let your imagination take off!

WHAT WILL YOU DO NEXT?

Before continuing to the next chapter, take the following steps toward your dream of living and working abroad:

- Prepare an international resume that can be tailored to specific positions.
- Have your resume translated by a language or cultural expert to be sure that it meets the needs of the hiring organization.
- Prepare a sample cover letter that can be tailored to specific international positions.
- Create a success portfolio.
- Consider enrolling in additional classes to brush up on desirable skills for working globally.
- Apply for an internship or create your own to fill in the gaps in your international experience.

6

Get Ahead—Interview!

When it comes to the international interview, you can expect to be asked anything and everything, with the possible exception of whether or not you've had a sex-change operation.

—Cherie, director of international human resources

Everything you've done up to this point has set the stage for your international employment interview. Congratulate yourself for making it this far in the process of landing your dream job abroad! Interviewing is one of the most challenging, yet potentially the most rewarding, hurdles of your global job search.

But as happy as you will be, and rightfully should be, to get an international interview, there's always the potential for an unsuccessful outcome. Only by preparing yourself as much as possible ahead of time can you hope to land your dream job abroad. In this chapter, you will discover how to present yourself during an international interview, how to distinguish yourself from your competition, how to respond to questions asked by the interviewer, and how to follow up once the interview is over.

HOW SHOULD I PREPARE FOR THE OVERSEAS JOB INTERVIEW?

Once your interview has been arranged, review your success portfolio to get an observer's perspective on how you qualify for a particular global position. Think about what you have to offer and how the organization will benefit by hiring you out of all the other candidates. Decide what it is you want the interviewer to know about you and plan your strategy to make sure you get that information across. Focus not only on your work accomplishments but also on your personal attributes. What will make you a desirable employee when working abroad?

Anticipate questions your interviewer might ask and prepare your own questions for the interviewer. Role-play interview scenarios and practice responding to uncomfortable questions with your mentor or another friend.

Employers often look for continuity in dates of employment. If you have gaps in your work history, be prepared to address questions about them.

WHAT SHOULD I WEAR?

Choose your clothing for the interview carefully. You'll want to wear an outfit that's comfortable and one in which you feel confident. Roger uses this approach in his workplace. On the days when he anticipates conflict at work, he wears his "don't mess with me" tie. It gives him the confidence he needs to work through difficult situations. I'm not suggesting that you go into your interview with a "don't mess with me" attitude, but do choose clothing that gives you that extra self-assurance.

Your overall objective should be to wear clothing that gives you a polished and professional appearance. Always err on the side of formality if you're unsure of cultural and business norms. You can always dress down as your host suggests, but you can't dress up once you discover that you're too casually dressed at an interview.

Naturally, you'll want to wear clothing that is comfortable, fits you well, and is age appropriate. Since you don't want to be conspicuous or easily ridiculed, avoid loud colors or prints. The color of your clothing also makes a statement that can differ, depending on the culture. For example, white is traditionally associated with mourning throughout the Far East, so avoid wearing a white outfit to an interview with an Asian employer.

On preliminary visits to the employer's office, pay attention to other people in the organization and note how they dress for work. But remember that the world and culture change quickly. Be observant of changes in business dress codes and select your clothing accordingly.

HOW CAN I DISTINGUISH MYSELF FROM THE COMPETITION?

With the international job interview, you've been invited to show your stuff. You're ready to make your dream of working overseas a reality. Of course, you may be nervous heading into an interview for a job you want badly. But if you've done your homework and conducted informational interviews, the knowledge you've gained will give you confidence. Your goal is to leverage this information into a job offer.

You want to stand out among all the applicants vying for an international position. Chances are, once you've gotten this far in the application process, your credentials are comparable to the competition's. What can you do, then, to stay indelibly in the mind of the interviewer long after you've walked out the door? Here are a few suggestions:

Show Initiative

Showing initiative is not the same as boasting about your achievements or putting yourself above those who helped you succeed. Showing initiative, in the context of the international job interview, means showing that you've prepared for the interview. Jack, a material superintendent for an American oil company abroad, explains:

> Prospective employees should come well prepared for interviews. I have been on recruiting trips where we have interviewed 10 to 15 people a day. After talking to that many people, it is very difficult to put a face to a name and remember who each individual is. It will help the prospective employees if they do something out of the ordinary. For example, I was interviewing people in the Philippines for warehousing positions. One fellow said, "I'm ready to work right away," and he reached in his bag, pulled out a McMaster-Carr catalog, and laid it on the table. This catalog is used in most oil companies overseas for reference. The fact that he had taken the initiative to bring it to the interview made him stand out, and he got the job.

Do your homework. Think about what you can do to distinguish yourself from the competition. Read up on the industry, organization, and key players. Beyond learning about the culture and mission of the company, find out what recent challenges and successes it has experienced. Become familiar with sensitive areas and touch on them gingerly.

Have a Good Icebreaker

Now that you know the value of icebreakers, choose one that might work in your particular interview. Jack explains how another prospective employee broke the ice: "He stopped halfway through the interview and asked, 'How am I doing so far? Am I coming on too strong?' This icebreaker made him stand out, and he also got the job."

Such an icebreaker might not work as well with Asian recruiters, who appreciate more indirect styles of communication. It pays to be perceptive and gauge what approach will work best for you with each particular interviewer.

Tell Your Story

When we bought our first house, our real estate agent explained how he intended to pitch us to the seller. He described our personalities, our lifestyle, and our personal interests. He made certain to touch on the areas of compatibility between us and the seller. In our case, those areas included a love of pets, as evidenced by our great dog, Gypsy. Our agent helped us stand out among the swarm of prospective buyers. By the end of his presentation, the seller felt comfortable enough to accept our offer.

In the same way, the international job interview gives you a chance to tell a story—your story (just as your CV allows you to write a synopsis of your life story). Throughout the interview, you'll want to paint a vivid picture in the mind of the interviewer about who you are and how you're different from other applicants.

Be Kind

It's a sad commentary on our global culture, perhaps, but there's a simple way today to stand out in a crowd of job applicants: Be caring, kind, and compassionate in your business and social dealings. Unfortunately, too many people are not. Sure, you want the job overseas. But if you try to get it by bad-mouthing the competition, you only make yourself look bad.

M ISTAKES TO AVOID

An American job applicant interviewing for an international position needs to know his or her audience. An American employer and, say, a European employer undoubtedly have the same goal—hiring the right person for the job. Yet, their expectations of you in the job interview may be vastly different. My former boss from England observed that Americans are very good at marketing and packaging themselves when it comes to job interviews. Since he had hired me, I was about to offer a humble thanks in reply. Then he added: "This makes it extremely difficult to get under the veneer to find out who the person really is!" I managed to choke back my thanks just in time.

What's an international job applicant to do? After all, haven't you been coached to create snazzy marketing tools as part of a professional image? It's critical to self-preservation in the applicant-eat-applicant job jungle, isn't it? Well, yes and no. Naturally, you needed to have credentials, relevant work experience, and professional marketing materials to get an international employer's attention in the first place. Now that you have, it's up to you to reveal the substance behind the initial presentation. Make it easy for the interviewer to know you and your character. While your marketing package may command attention, you'll want to avoid coming across as too slick yourself. If you appear to give canned responses to questions, you might leave the interviewer wondering who you really are. The best thing to do is to be natural in how you communicate and display an open, positive attitude. While your role is reversed from the informational interview—you won't be asking the questions—your preparation can help you direct the conversation to ensure that the interviewer learns exactly what you want him or her to know.

Let's look at some of the cultural differences you may encounter between North American interviewers and their European, Latin American, and Asian counterparts. Here are some typical mistakes North American interviewees make and how to avoid them:

Getting Down to Business Too Quickly

In Chapter 3, we discussed how North Americans like to get down to business quickly during an interview, without taking time to build rapport first. Remember that the first few moments of your international job interview are a wonderful way for you and the interviewer to break the ice, relax, and help each other get comfortable. The preliminary conversation helps the interviewer get to know you apart from the business discussion that is to follow. Use this time to your advantage.

Instead of discussing yourself to begin the conversation, offer your observations (preferably positive) about the local culture, perhaps regarding some of the sights you've taken in and foods you've eaten since arriving. Your interviewer will want to know that you can adapt to the foreign culture easily. Eating the local food shows that you're adventurous and willing to try something new. Ask informal questions that demonstrate your interest in your new surroundings. Avoid such controversial subjects as politics, religion, and sex, even if they are in the news.

Boasting of Personal Accomplishments

Self-praise is appreciated little by interviewers in many Asian and European cultures. Keep in mind the perception of my English boss. If you're as good as you think you are, your credentials, accomplishments, and personal references will speak for themselves. The interviewer wants to learn who you are as a *person,* not just what you've achieved. When you draw too much attention to your individual achievements, you risk creating an impression of arrogance and bravado. Your interviewer may think you are inconsiderate or a "Lone Ranger." Tone down your achievements in your conversation with foreign employers. By all means, let the interviewer know what role you played in an organization's success, but stress that you were more of a contributor than an "architect."

Lacking Deference

We mainstream North Americans like to get on a first-name basis with others as soon as possible. It's a mark of our casualness, friendliness, and informality. Yet, in many other cultures, using a first name is a surefire way to alienate the other person. Unless you have been invited to refer to the other person by his or her first name, you're liable to come across as disrespectful of that person's title, rank, and status within an organization.

Even if you know better than to jump to a first-name basis with your interviewer, it's easy to blow it when it comes to foreign etiquette. For instance, what do you do with a business card that's been presented to you?

Do you read it or do you quickly put it in your pocket with nary a glance? If you pocket the card in Japan, you've just committed a major business blunder. It's considered extremely rude not to read business cards carefully and pay proper respect to a person's name and title.

You should show deference during the international interview by respecting the interviewer's age, avoiding personal questions, and using appropriate body language. In the United States we value direct eye contact. We interpret it as self-confidence and openness. When a speaker doesn't maintain direct eye contact, we often assume that he or she lacks confidence or perhaps has something to hide. In some countries, though, the exact opposite is true. Not knowing the appropriate behavior can lead to some awkward moments during an interview.

Assuming English-Speaking Interviewers Will Understand You

We sometimes tend to think that if we share a common language with another person that our values will also be the same. This is a false assumption, however, that can land you in serious trouble during an international job interview. When my former boss came to the United States from England, he created quite a stir by asking a female office manager if he could borrow a rubber. What he wanted was an eraser; what he got was frosty silence. Remember, even if the words are the same, they sometimes have completely different meanings in other cultures. If you've done your research about your host country, you can at least minimize your look of shock when you hear familiar words used differently.

Using Inappropriate Humor

We often use humor when we're trying to break the ice. Humor *can* diffuse tension during uncomfortable situations. But we can't assume that a foreign interviewer will always understand our humor. If you make a joke that is over the other person's head, or worse is offensive, then you've only managed to exacerbate everyone's discomfort. Using humor across cultures is a potential minefield of misinterpretations and misunderstandings.

Certain words (*rubber*, for example) can have very different meanings in different languages and an unintended impact. Even if your interviewer understands and speaks English, cultural references can be confusing. For example, my American-born Russian professor, obviously fluent in Russian, told our class about the time he rode a city bus in Moscow. A small group had gathered to read a cartoon in the local newspaper. Everyone was laughing hysterically and having such a good time that my professor decided to join them. He read the cartoon, understood every single word, and still failed to get the joke. He simply didn't know enough about the popular culture.

WHAT TYPE OF QUESTIONS CAN I EXPECT?

Once again, that depends on who's asking the questions. If you're interviewing with an American employer, you're already familiar with the type of questions interviewers love to ask. These questions include: "Why do you want to work for our company?" "Why should I hire you?" "What are your strengths and weaknesses?" Beyond the standard questions, let's look at the kinds of questions that often come up in international interviews.

As the former director of international human resources at Westin Hotels and Resorts, Cherie interviewed candidates for positions overseas. She also managed international recruiters. In searching for the right person for a position, Cherie focused on how well the person would adjust to living and working abroad. She asked questions designed to reveal whether candidates could adapt to a cultural change. She elaborates:

> I didn't need people who were out to change the world or know-it-alls. Skills and second-language fluency were secondary. What I wanted was a person who could respect different beliefs and lifestyles. We needed someone who could accept how things are done within another culture and who understood that one culture isn't better than another, only different.

Gail worked as a civilian employee for the U.S. Department of Defense in Germany. Like Cherie, her interviewer presented a series of scenarios meant to determine how well she would respond to unfamiliar or uncomfortable cultural interactions.

Let's look at some possible questions you might face when applying for work overseas, particularly with an American-owned company. Your interviewer might be looking for the following qualities, as outlined in Chapter 1:

Adaptability
Sample Questions:
- You show up for your first day of work overseas. The office in which you were expecting to work is still under construction and an office assistant is nowhere to be found. How would you handle this situation?
- Imagine the same scenario, but now it's two weeks later. How would you cope?
- Have you ever had a similar work experience that tested your ability to be flexible? What did you do in that situation?

Acceptance of Differences
Sample Question:
- You're having lunch with colleagues abroad who have ordered for you. You find the meal especially tasty and ask what it is you're eating. There's a long pause. A business associate fills you in: That tasty dish you're eating is raw monkey brains. You're then asked to sample some snake blood. Describe your reaction.

Positive Attitude, Patience, and Perseverance
Sample Questions:
- How have you managed in a workplace relationship with a difficult person? How did you feel and what did you do about the situation?
- Describe a customer-service situation in which your needs were not met. How did you handle it?

Ability to Communicate across Cultures
Sample Question:
- Describe a time when you couldn't understand another person because of a language or cultural difference. What did you do to facilitate communication? How successful were you in reaching mutual understanding?

Ability to Fail

Sample Questions:

- Describe a time when you were not successful in meeting your goals or the goals set by your supervisor. What was the outcome of that experience?
- Describe a time when you felt excluded in some way from a larger group. What was the impact on you and how did you respond to the situation?

Sense of Humor

Sample Questions:

- Give an example of how you used humor to break the ice in an uncomfortable situation.
- Talk about an embarrassing moment you had and how you handled it.

Self-Reliance

Sample Questions:

- Describe self-directed work projects for which you've been responsible. How did you manage them?
- You've just flown into a foreign country, and you don't speak the language. You're late for an important business appointment. You hop in a cab and give the address of your meeting. Your cab driver shakes his head and begins gesticulating wildly. You have no idea what he's trying to tell you, and you have to get to your appointment right away. What do you do?

Curiosity

Sample Questions

- You're supervising a multicultural staff on international assignment. You recommend a promotion for a staff member, but the person turns down the opportunity. How would you respond in this situation?
- You overhear a conversation among several employees in your office. You hear a lot of laughing, but you don't know why because you don't speak their language. What do you do?

Outgoingness

Sample Questions:

- One of the most difficult challenges in relocating overseas is making new friends. How would you go about this?
- Describe a recent friendship you made. How did you meet the person and strike up an acquaintance?

Motivation

Sample Questions:

- Not everyone you know may support your decision to live and work abroad. How would you explain your motivation for wanting to relocate overseas?
- Why do you want to work abroad?

Trust

Sample Questions:

- Describe a situation in which you built trust with a person who was different from you in some way. What was the result?
- How did you rebuild trust that had been broken, either because of something you or another person had done?

Acculturation

Sample Questions:

- What type of housing and amenities would you prefer when living abroad?
- You usually enjoy an early dinner and go to bed before 11 p.m. Once overseas, however, you find that your assignment often requires you to socialize into the early morning hours. How would you cope with this situation?

Cultural Understanding

Sample Question:

- Describe the last time you found yourself in an uncomfortable situation at work. How did you handle it?

If you're applying for work with a foreign-owned company, however, all bets are off as to the type of questions you could be asked. The unpredictable and sometimes intrusive questions asked by foreign employers shouldn't come as too great a surprise when you consider foreign employment ads. Mike describes the kind of ads he saw when working in Asia: "The want ads in the newspaper... clearly state that a company is looking for a '25- to 30- year-old, good-looking woman, unmarried, with a pleasant demeanor.' That and a smile would get you jail time in the United States."

So don't be surprised, then, if an interviewer in a foreign country thinks nothing of asking such questions as:

- How old are you?
- Are you married?
- Have you ever been divorced?
- Have you ever been arrested?
- How much money do you make in your current job?
- What does your husband or wife do for a living?
- How many children do you have?
- How old are your children?
- What political party do you belong to?
- Tell me about your parents and grandparents.
- Where do you live now?
- What's your religion?

Of course, context is everything. Interviewers for foreign-owned companies ask these questions because they can—because those questions are acceptable in many foreign cultures.

HOW SHOULD I RESPOND?

How you respond to a foreign interviewer's questions is up to you. Be honest and reveal what you feel comfortable revealing. If you're prepared for the uncomfortable questions, the interviewer won't see you sweat. But allow yourself a moment to consider how you want to respond, and think before you speak.

If you'd rather not answer a question directly, you might be able to get away with pretending not to understand. Teacher and author Bruce Feiler described this strategy in his book *Learning to Bow*. A new teacher in Japan, Bruce was asked at his welcome party, "Do you like sex?" Clearly uncomfortable, Bruce thought for a moment before smiling and answering, "Yes, I like sushi very much."

If the interviewer's questions have made you uncomfortable, you can ask your own questions to gain knowledge, clarify your understanding, and even stall for time while you decide how to answer. When you ask questions, be sure to listen carefully to the answers you receive. Not only does this action demonstrate respect but it also gives you information that can help you engage in a fruitful conversation.

WHAT KINDS OF QUESTIONS SHOULD I ASK?

The interview is a time for you to discover whether or not a job is, in fact, a good fit for you. I knew before I left for a teaching assignment in Egypt that some aspects of the job didn't sound right. I chose not to ask more questions during my interview, because I was afraid the answers would only confirm my underlying misgivings about making the trip. It turned out that my apprehension was well founded. I encountered a lot of problems with that particular venture. In retrospect, I should have asked more questions up front. In all likelihood, I would have taken the job regardless of the answers, because I knew it was a short-term assignment. But by asking the questions ahead of time, at least I would have known what to expect and planned accordingly.

Here are a few questions you may want to ask during your international job interview:

- Do you handle the paperwork needed for my work permit and business visa? What about the paperwork needed for my family?
- Will my salary be paid in U.S. dollars or the local currency?
- What adjustment is made for cost-of-living variables? What does it include?
- Will I need to pay foreign local income tax?
- In addition to the salary, what else does the compensation package include (health-care benefits, bonuses, paid vacation, sick leave)?
- Does the organization pay relocation costs? What expenses will be included (airline travel, shipping)?

- What is the length of the contract?
- Does the company pay for annual trips to the United States?
- What types of housing arrangements are available? What contribution does the company offer toward housing?
- Is a car provided with this position? What kind of car? Who pays for the insurance, parking fees, gas, and maintenance?
- What can you tell me about the local schools? Does the company contribute to the cost of tuition?
- What job opportunities are available for my partner who will accompany me abroad?
- How good is the medical care in the area? Will the company pay for care from a doctor or medical facility of my choice? Will the company pay for medical care in another country if needed?
- Tell me about safety and security concerns in the area. Does the company provide protection, such as a driver and car service, in hostile environments?
- Does the company provide support in insurance-claim processing or legal matters as needed?

Use your judgment in deciding which of these questions to ask. If you are offered a position, the answers to the questions will help you decide whether or not to accept it. It's generally not advisable to bring up salary expectations until you've been offered a job, however.

FOLLOWING UP AFTER YOUR INTERNATIONAL JOB INTERVIEW

At the end of your international job interview, find out about the next step in the hiring process. Ask how soon you can expect a decision. You may learn that the interviewer has several other candidates to interview or that he or she will be taking a vacation before making a decision. In any case, ask, so you'll know what to expect.

Follow up afterward with a written note thanking the interviewer for his or her time. Use the note as an opportunity to reiterate your enthusiasm about working for the organization and as a reminder of how you can contribute to the company's overall success.

If you haven't heard anything by the time a hiring decision is expected, take the initiative and follow up with a call to the interviewer. Never assume that another person has been hired or that the organization isn't interested in offering you a position just because you haven't been contacted.

WHAT WILL YOU DO NEXT?

Before continuing on to the next chapter, take these steps to reach your dream of living and working abroad:

- Enhance your understanding of different cultural groups in preparation for international interviews.
- Role-play international interview scenarios with a mentor or a member of your success support group.
- Prepare a list of questions to ask during international interviews.
- Practice responding to uncomfortable interview questions.

7

expatriate

Get There—Succeed!

One of the best pieces of advice I could give to anyone going global is to "get it in writing."

—*Mike, expatriate*

This chapter addresses the question of how to negotiate an international job contract in today's global marketplace. You'll find critical information on how to secure visas and work permits, prepare for your relocation abroad, and deal with culture shock.

WHAT DO I NEED TO KNOW ABOUT VISAS AND WORK PERMITS?

Most important, you'd better have the proper documents before you start working abroad—that is, unless you don't mind risking deportation and paying fines. Passports, visas, and work permits are official legal documents that allow you to enter, reside in, and work in a particular country. The entry requirements for short-term travelers and expatriates vary considerably from one country to the next. Your best bet is to contact the consulate or embassy of the country in which you wish to travel and work and request current entry information. These agencies can tell you the rules and restrictions about working in a particular country and can explain the procedures for obtaining the necessary documents.

Typically, for long-term assignments, your overseas employer will manage the immigration process for you. Having your employer handle the paperwork is a lot easier than trying to do it yourself. If you do have to handle the application yourself, be aware that the process can be a lengthy and frustrating one. You'll need to demonstrate that you will have adequate financial resources while in the host country. You'll also have to ensure that you won't be taking away any local resident's employment.

Let the company that's hiring you handle the paperwork whenever possible. Companies that have already hired others for overseas assignments will know the ropes. They will be familiar with the immigration authorities and agencies, which will be more likely to expedite your travel documents. The employer can vouch for you financially and ensure that you have specialized skills—meaning that you won't be taking away employment from local residents. In short, having the employer take care of immigration matters saves you time, money, and heartache.

What if you're asked to go overseas sooner than you had planned, and you don't even have a passport? Not to worry. Expediter companies can usually get you the document in 24 hours if needed. Of course, this service comes with a hefty price tag. An expediter typically charges up to $150—and that's in addition to the passport agency's $35 fee for rush delivery and $60 for the passport itself ($40 for a renewal). Still, it's reassuring to know that you can make it overseas in a hurry if you have to.

W HAT'S OPEN FOR NEGOTIATION IN AN INTERNATIONAL CONTRACT?

People working abroad in the heady days of the 1960s and 1970s could just about write their own tickets. Salaries and relocation benefits were generous. Since then, international companies have attempted to reduce relocation costs. It's easy to understand why: It now costs $50,000 on average to move an expatriate family. A failed overseas assignment can cost a company as much as $350,000.

Consequently, international organizations have tightened their budgets in several ways. First, rather than send an American overseas, a company might employ foreign nationals. This effort has the wide support of host countries, especially in regions of high unemployment. A company might also present an overseas job as a career booster, persuading an employee to accept the position, even with a modest compensation package.

Despite these trends, it's not always easy for companies to find qualified candidates who are willing to work abroad—a point in your favor. There's almost always room for negotiation when the company believes that you're the right candidate. Before negotiating, though, you need to find out how desirable your skills are for the overseas job market and how badly the organization wants to hire you.

You also have to know your priorities: Which of your employment and relocation needs are absolutely critical, which are important but not critical, and which are of no concern at all. You will be strongest in the negotiations when you know your "walk-away point." As Jack tells it: "When I interviewed, I was offered a single-status job overseas. Although I wanted the job, I turned down the contract, because I did not want to go without my wife. My employer came back almost immediately with a revised, married-status offer, so some negotiating is possible."

ELEMENTS OF THE COMPENSATION PACKAGE

Overseas compensation packages vary considerably, depending on international hiring practices at any given moment, your position in the organization, and your overseas destination. Of course, compensation levels also vary widely among voluntary, government, and corporate organizations. Here is what companies commonly offer in compensation to globe-trotting employees before, during, and after the international assignment. Use this list as the basis of your negotiations with an international employer:

Before Departure
Exploratory Trip   Most large corporations will offer you the chance to visit an overseas location before finalizing your international contract. Include your partner in this investigative trip so you can both see firsthand what the destination is like. Plan on staying a week or so to check out basics such as housing, cost of living, transportation, and schools. Typically, the company will hire someone to show you around the area and answer your questions.

For Harriet, who was accompanying her husband on his overseas assignment in Hong Kong, the exploratory trip was very helpful. Although the visit was brief, it gave her "an important glimpse at what life might be like in a very different environment. . . . They met with us and gave us a tour of Hong Kong and a lot of orientation materials about local customs, shopping, services, and transportation."

For the exploratory trip, companies will either give you an allowance and expect you to make your own travel arrangements or will make the arrangements for you. Some companies have begun using economy (coach) fares to reduce costs. If you've ever traveled internationally, then you know that flying in coach class can be uncomfortable. Do what it takes to secure a business-class ticket to your overseas destination.

Automobile Disposal   If it's cost-effective for you to dispose of your automobile before moving abroad, do so. The company will encourage it. If you can't get a fair price for your car, it's possible that the company will cover the difference.

Shipping   A company will usually give you an allowance for the cost of shipping your household goods and furnishings to your foreign residence. In some cases, this allowance is capped by weight or volume. Mike's international contract had "an either/or clause, where the company would pay for a full container of belongings to be shipped from and back to the United States, or you could opt for a minimal shipping package of personal belongings (clothes and kitchen stuff), and they would pay for a certain amount of furniture for your apartment. Or they would pay the extra to get you a furnished apartment. It all depended on what you wanted." You'll have to figure out which arrangement is most cost-effective for you. Keep in mind the cost of placing your possessions in storage while you're working abroad. Weigh your options carefully before you negotiate.

Cross-Cultural Preparation   It's in the hiring organization's best interests for you to succeed in your overseas assignment. Therefore, it makes good business sense for companies to include cross-cultural preparation in your compensation package. The NFTC reports that 70 percent of member companies provide cross-cultural preparation, up from 61 percent the year before.

Curiously, 33 percent of eligible employees decline this assistance. But if you think that such preparation isn't worth negotiating for, think again. The majority of expatriates I queried stated that if they had it to do over again, they would learn more about the language and culture of their host countries before moving abroad. Culture shock is not a fabrication. Without the tools to manage it effectively, you and your family might end up returning to the United States prematurely. Why not make the most of your stay abroad? Take advantage of the opportunity to learn as much as you can about the local population and your host country before traveling abroad.

During Your International Assignment

Orientation Services The hiring organization will want you to acclimate to your new location as quickly as possible and will usually bring in a firm to help you get settled. In Harriet's case, she was invited to a coffee gathering, at which she was introduced to other newly arrived expatriate wives. She went on several outings with the group, including a walking tour of key shopping districts, to become familiar with the surrounding area. Generally, orientation firms can also plug you into additional associations of interest to you and can offer family assistance as the need arises.

Salary While your salary is but one part of your overall compensation package, it's an important part. Through your preliminary research, you now have some idea of the typical salary range offered for the position you're seeking overseas (62 percent of NFTC members base their compensation packages for international assignments on home-country standards). If you aren't sure of the salary range, it's time to contact people in your personal network for advice. Do a thorough investigation before you begin negotiations.

To make an informed decision, you'll need to know whether you'll be paid in U.S. dollars or local currency. If you're paid in local currency, you'll be in for quite a shock if the bottom falls out of the economy (as it did in Brazil and Asia). Devaluation of the local currency can cut your salary by half—or more—overnight.

Income Tax Equalization By itself, your salary figure doesn't mean a whole lot without taking into account the taxes you'll need to pay on it.

Often, the company that hires you will equalize your tax payments abroad to match what you would pay in the United States. This means that you continue to pay U.S. taxes on your base salary, while your company handles the foreign taxes. Alternatively, the company might pay you in local currency with the understanding that you will accept responsibility for paying all taxes at home and abroad. Consult with your tax accountant for advice on making the best financial decision for you and your family.

Health Coverage While health coverage may not be a negotiable item in your international contract, it's important enough to warrant your full attention. It's the rare organization that doesn't provide at least some basic health coverage for its employees. Nevertheless, ask for full details of what is and isn't covered in your company policy so you know exactly what to expect.

It's good to know if the company has an emergency medical evacuation plan in place. Jack states: "Our company had a contract to provide evacuation, by a medically equipped Lear Jet, in any case in which one of their employees required immediate medical attention. To my knowledge this was never required, but it was comforting to know it was available if needed. With quick and easy air transportation, all but the most urgent medical care can be obtained from one's host country."

Hardship Premium If the company views your overseas assignment as a particularly difficult one, expect a "hardship premium" in compensation. What constitutes a hardship environment? It could be a location that is isolated or one with high security risks, an unstable economy, few community resources, poor communication systems, health risks, inferior schools, poor medical facilities, or curtailed freedoms.

Cost-of-Living Allowance In addition to income tax equalization, organizations compute the difference in daily living costs between your home and host countries. If food, clothing, transportation, and other such services cost more in the host country, the company should make up the difference.

Housing Allowance International employees often look for housing on their preliminary, exploratory trip abroad. If you aren't able to locate suitable permanent housing on this trip, your organization should house you in temporary quarters, usually at company expense, until you do.

Employee housing allowances vary. On Mike's assignment, "If you had rented an apartment in your home country, the company did an 'equivalent-plus-local-conditions' upcharge and paid that much against your host-country housing. If you owned a home in the United States, the company just paid the whole cost of host-country housing at your grade level. For me, a 'C-band' employee, that translated to about $10,000 per month in Hong Kong. I could contribute more if I wanted a classier place."

In countries with a large expatriate population, you'll often find many American families living in the same general location—often near the schools that their children attend. That doesn't necessarily mean you have to live in the same neighborhood, but you'll enjoy more community services and family support if you do.

If you own a home in the United States, most organizations will also pay for a property management firm to take care of it while you're abroad. This service includes leasing the property, collecting payment, and protecting it against damage.

Transportation Allowance In some cases, an international employer will include a transportation allowance in your compensation package. If you will be living in a dangerous location, the employer may even provide a chauffeured car service. In any event, it doesn't hurt to ask if a car, gas, and maintenance expenses, or the cost of public transportation, will be part of your overall benefits.

School Tuition Most companies understand parents' concerns about their children's education while abroad. As a result, your employer may contribute to tuition costs for your children's schooling.

Home Leave Expect your company to finance the cost of an annual home leave for your entire family. This benefit enables you to maintain ties with your community of friends and relatives. You may be able to negotiate a leave for another vacation destination instead of a return trip home.

Job Placement for Married Partners Human resources professionals report that the loss of spousal income or career opportunities is one of the chief reasons candidates ultimately turn down international offers. Bill, a former human resources director in Indonesia, explains the dilemma: "My company would contact other American companies abroad to find work for the employee's spouse whenever possible. But this would require the company to sponsor the spouse, and in some countries, like Indonesia, they could only get so many visas."

If finding an overseas position for your spouse is likely to be difficult, you might be able to negotiate a lump-sum payment to make up for the lost income. Alternatively, you could negotiate for a higher company contribution to housing or tuition costs. Even if your partner is able to find a position overseas, you'll need to weigh carefully the potential long-term impact of the move on his or her career.

After Your International Assignment

Return Travel Expenses   You wouldn't really accept any international job offer that came with a one-way ticket, would you? Just checking.

Return Shipping Costs   Your negotiations should always include the cost of shipping your belongings back home when your assignment is finished. Apply the same rules for travel, shipping, and storage expenses at the end of your stay as you did before leaving home.

Interim Housing   You may not be able to move back into your previous home immediately when you return. In this case, you'll need to have your employer pick up the tab for temporary housing arrangements. Make sure you negotiate for this scenario.

Completion Bonus   Not every company provides a completion bonus for the international job assignment. In fact, 72 percent of member companies surveyed by the NFTC do not. If your hiring organization doesn't offer one, put it on the negotiating table. The bonus can amount to 10 to 20 percent of your base salary, paid on an annual basis or in one lump sum when your assignment terminates. The completion bonus is sometimes coupled with a clause requiring you to work for the company in the United States upon your return, generally for six months to a year.

Repatriation Preparation Even organizations that provide predeparture training often fail to recognize the importance of preparing expatriate families for the return home. Yet processing your overseas experiences is a vital part of easing your transition back home. Be sure to consider this training in your negotiations. (We'll look at reentry preparation in more detail in Chapter 9.)

TAKING CARE OF BUSINESS BEFORE LEAVING

The details of making the move overseas can be overwhelming. If your international assignment requires it, you may even find yourself having to leave ahead of your family—thus leaving your partner to deal with the minutiae of the move.

For Elena, "The logistics of moving abroad were a hassle and enormously complicated—and therefore tiring and stressful. There were so many decisions to make before our move, such as what to do with our home, vehicles, rental properties, and pets."

One way to minimize the stress of relocation is to take the time in advance to make good decisions and plans. Make a checklist of items that will require your attention before leaving. Here are a few places to start:

Mail Delivery

To ensure uninterrupted mail delivery, fill out a change-of-address form at your local post office. Note that the post office will only forward magazines for a couple of months, though. You're better off notifying magazines directly with your change of address.

Also give your new overseas address to friends, family, and anyone else with whom you expect to correspond regularly. That way, they will know how to reach you directly—the postal service won't have to forward their mail to your overseas address.

But what if you don't have a permanent address when you first go overseas? If at all possible, designate a specific location where your mail can be sent. This might be the home of an American friend, who can then forward your mail overseas at regular intervals. Naturally, you should reimburse your friend for the cost of mailing. More preferably, designate a location abroad where you can first receive your mail, even if it's not your permanent address. Check to see if your overseas bank, post office, or employer would accept mail for you until you get settled.

Whether you have a permanent address abroad or not, be prepared for delays in mail delivery. As Harriet explains: "We had a lot of problems getting our mail regularly in the beginning. It took lots of phone calls and faxes back to the United States to get it straightened out."

Money Issues

Advance planning is particularly important when it comes to money and banking. Be sure that your credit cards can be used overseas, and check out the rates and surcharges. Harriet warns about the perils of mailing payments and statements internationally: "If your credit cards are issued by banks in the United States, finding out the balance due and getting payments in on time takes some careful planning."

Remember, too, says Harriet: "You still have financial commitments in the United States that have to be taken care of. We tried to have as many of our monetary transactions as possible (paying our mortgage, for instance) done by automatic, electronic transfer and arranged this before leaving the United States." The bottom line is, the fewer payments you have to mail home while overseas, the better you'll sleep at night.

En route to your destination, Cherie recommends bringing 20 or 30 one-dollar bills to cover tips. You should also bring a small amount of the local currency, so you won't need to change money immediately upon arrival. If you have a major credit card in good standing, you can always get cash quickly at automatic teller machines. Finally, it's smart to bring along traveler's checks for unexpected expenses.

Paying Taxes

Paying your taxes is certainly a money issue—but one deserving of its own discussion. Whether you live at home or abroad, the IRS has a vested interest in your annual earned income. In fact, the IRS is *so* interested in your income that it even employs full-time staff in many U.S. embassies just to dispense forms, handle problems, and assist in the preparation of expatriate tax returns. At last check, the IRS had such employees in Bonn, London, Mexico City, Paris, Rome, Singapore, and Tokyo.

According to the IRS, if you are a U.S. citizen or resident alien who lives and works abroad, you may be able to exclude part or all of your foreign earnings from your taxable income. To qualify, you must meet the "bona fide residence or physical presence test." Basically, you must have a "tax home" in a foreign country, meaning that you are present in the country for at least 330 full days during any 12 consecutive months. If you meet this requirement, in the year 2000, you may exclude up to $76,000 from your taxable earned income. This amount will increase by $2,000 a year until 2002. For further information, contact your accountant or request a free "Tax Guide for U.S. Citizens and Resident Aliens Abroad" (Publication 54) from 800/829-3676 or www.irs.ustreas.gov.

Doctor and Dentist Appointments

You know how long it can take to get a doctor or dentist appointment under normal circumstances. Give yourself plenty of time, then, to set up appointments for yourself and your family before you head overseas. Let your doctors know that you'll be traveling and living outside the country so that they can plan for your visit accordingly. Find out what, if any, immunizations you'll need, then allow enough time for a series of shots. Be aware that some immunization series can take up to six months.

Be sure to bring copies of your medical records to your overseas destination. That way, in the event of an emergency, you won't have to rely on your physician and the postal service to make sure you receive them. You'll also want to bring any prescription medication you take and copies of prescriptions.

Insurance and Health Care

Check your health, home, and auto insurance policies to determine if you will have adequate coverage while traveling and living abroad. Of course, your international employer will be your best source of information about the company's health insurance policy. If the organization is unable to answer your questions or concerns, contact the insurance company directly. Keep copies of your policies with you for fast and easy access should you need them overseas.

Find out ahead of time what you can expect in medical services at your overseas destination. Perhaps your organization employs its own doctor, which will make it easier and faster for you to receive medical care when you need it. You hope that neither you nor your family members will require the services of a physician or hospital during your time abroad, but find out what services and facilities are available.

School Transfer

If you have children in school, meet with their teachers as soon as possible to notify them of your upcoming move abroad. If your departure is to take place near the end of the academic year, find out what requirements your children must still meet to complete their current grade levels. Ask for copies of any records that will be needed to place your children in overseas schools.

Supplies and Provisions

Even with the best of intentions to adapt to the local culture, at times you'll long for some of your favorite treats from home. Realize, though, that you might not be able to find them in your host country. Use your exploratory trip to visit grocery stores, drugstores, and department stores to see what goods are and aren't available. If you know what you're going to miss ahead of time, you can take your favorites with you or arrange to have friends send you care packages occasionally.

But it won't just be treats that you will miss overseas. You might even have trouble finding the essentials. In Japan, for instance, people are generally smaller than Americans. If you're tall or large, you might have a hard time finding Japanese clothing and shoes that fit you. Use your exploratory trip to investigate such problems, then stock up on essentials before you leave home.

PREPARING FOR CULTURE SHOCK

In preparing for your adventure abroad, plan on dealing with culture shock, regardless of your level of professional experience. Culture shock doesn't affect everyone, at least not necessarily to the same degree. Nevertheless, you'll want to be prepared to cope with it, if and when it hits.

On my first trip outside the United States, I went to Egypt. At the time, I'd been teaching English as a second language to students from around the world for several years. I thought I knew everything I needed to know about culture shock. I had witnessed my students' reactions to living abroad: the initial euphoria at experiencing a totally new way of living and speaking; a letdown upon realizing that their familiar ways didn't always work in a new environment; increasing irritability—even hostility—as the frustration mounted; gradual willingness to accept new situations; and, finally, cultural adaptation.

When I got to Alexandria, I was the only one who thought I'd somehow manage to escape culture shock. My globetrotting colleagues simply sat back and, with a wink and a nod, waited for the fallout. When the shock hit me, it came fast and furious. The unrelenting desert heat, the pushing crowds, the threat of disease and illness, and dietary changes—all of this turned my small world upside down overnight. Alexandria, with its dilapidated buildings left untended, seemed to be a city on the verge of ruin. As I quickly discovered, knowing about culture shock intellectually is one thing, but experiencing it directly is another. Even if you're well traveled internationally, living abroad for either a short- or long-term stay can generate unexpected feelings of isolation and anxiety.

Jack has worked abroad most of his adult life. He knows culture shock firsthand. As a recruiter for overseas assignments, he's also seen others go through the experience. He comments:

> When people arrive on a foreign assignment, they know none of the things they take for granted at home. They don't know where anything is. They don't know where to eat. They don't know anyone. In short, they are completely lost. Most companies will ease an employee through this difficult period, but others do not. The new employee must often make his or her own way, and this can be traumatic. I have seen people who want to quit within the first week. I always advise them to give the job a chance and stick it out at least a month. Typically, by then they will have become acclimated to the new environment. If they wish to quit after that amount of time, OK. Some do, but most come to accept their new environment.

Developing your awareness of culture shock and its potential impact is the first step in overcoming it. A second step, and one of your best defenses, is to find out as much as possible about your host country and its culture before you go abroad. You may have already started your research when considering where you wanted to live abroad in the first place. Once you have your assignment, continue to research the country by reading interviews with people who have lived there, either as host nationals or expatriates. Get a flavor for the environment by reading literary accounts written by other travelers. If you have time to learn a little of the local language before you go, so much the better. Your goal is to make a gradual but smooth transition into your new location. When you have some background on the host country and an idea of what to expect beforehand, your transition will be easier. Here's a partial list of topics you might want to explore before you go:

- Weather and climate
- Geography
- Population statistics and demographics
- National holidays
- Language
- Government structure and politics
- Legal system and laws
- Military system
- National anthem
- Religions, religious ceremonies, and spiritual practices
- Famous landmarks and sites
- Popular figures, present and past
- Popular foods and dietary restrictions
- Meals, dining out, and tipping
- Popular sports, hobbies, and entertainment
- Television programs and movies
- The arts and museums
- Popular music
- Cultural and religious ceremonies
- Marriage and divorce practices
- Gift-giving practices
- Greetings and introductions
- Social taboos

- Postal system
- Shopping
- Hair care and other services
- Housing options
- Health-care services
- Banking
- Public and private transportation
- Dressing norms
- School systems
- School discipline
- Family roles
- Calendar year
- Business hours
- Business customs and practices

Think about your daily activities over a two-month period at home. Do you know how the same activities are handled in the host country? The more you can do to find out before moving abroad, the better.

You won't learn all the information on your list before you relocate. In fact, you may not even want to. After all, part of the joy of moving abroad is discovering some of this information by firsthand experience. Yet learning at least a little about a country's social, political, and economic norms before you arrive will help you adapt to the culture that much faster.

A third step you can take to minimize the effects of culture shock is to talk about your experiences, questions, and concerns. You may choose to speak with a host national who can give you an insider's perspective and perhaps shed some light on what you're feeling. By all means, disclose your feelings to family members and encourage them to do the same. That way, you can all help each other through the relocation process. You may choose to express yourself through journal writing. It will give you a safe emotional outlet and a way to vent your anger when needed.

Culture shock is one of the inherent risks of living and working overseas. You can take solace in knowing that most international travelers go through the same experience. When thinking of culture shock, I'm reminded of the Zen proverb that states, "The only way out is through." You can resist it, deny it, or openly fight it, but to get out of culture shock, you have to go through the stages that will bring you to cultural acceptance.

WHAT WILL YOU DO NEXT?

Before continuing to the next chapter, take these steps to reach your dream of living and working abroad. Here are a few places to start:

- Review the elements of an international compensation package. Determine your needs and priorities regarding compensation and benefits, including your "walk-away point."
- Make a list of your daily activities over a two-month period. Find out how these activities are handled in your host country.
- Learn as much as you can about the host country from research and interviews with people who live there.
- Make a list of everyone who should have your change of address and notify them.
- Complete a change-of-address form at your local post office.
- Designate a location for forwarding your mail.

8

Get Adjusted—
Acculturate!

Travel like Gandhi, with simple clothes, open eyes, and an uncluttered mind.
—Rick Steves, travel writer

You've made it! You've been offered a great international assignment, and you've negotiated a favorable contract. Now it's time to prove you can succeed in that assignment by adapting to the cultural norms and established business practices in your host country. Of course, you'll want to explore information about your host country in depth before your journey abroad. But, in this chapter, I offer a list of general language and cultural tips and advice about behavior that could get you into trouble if you're unaware or, worse, disinterested. I've also provided thumbnail sketches of business practices in 10 of the most popular areas for overseas employment.

GREETINGS AND INTRODUCTIONS

Informality is one of the distinguishing characteristics of American culture. Specifically, we Americans tend to overlook the importance that rank, status, and titles play in global interactions. We might call our international hosts by their first names, even mispronouncing them, before establishing trust and rapport. We might add a light touch on the arm or shoulder in an effort to seem warm, approachable, and friendly. Often, in cultures where formality rules, such gestures amount to coming on too strong, too familiar, and too fast.

I once introduced my English and Swedish bosses to an American college president—all males. Unfortunately, I had forgotten the American's tendency to greet people with a hug rather than a handshake, even at first introductions. As the American approached the Swedish man, the Swede extended his hand, which the American rebuffed in favor of an embrace. The Swede blushed deep red, kept his arms tightly at his side with hands clenched, and said nothing.

My English boss had been quietly observing the scene. I could see the wheels churning in his head. As the American approached, the Englishman took one step forward, extended his hand far out in front, and put his briefcase between himself and the American. The move worked. The Englishman got off with a handshake. You can be sure that once we were alone, my foreign bosses expressed their shock and disbelief about the encounter.

With this example in mind, make it easy for your international hosts to do business with you by following *their* norms in greetings and introductions. As you get to know each other better, the formality may relax a bit, but only after you've developed your relationship.

B USINESS CARDS

Business cards have cultural implications in the global marketplace. In Chapter 3, I mentioned the importance of presenting and receiving cards in a respectful manner when networking across cultures. As a general rule, the more highly rank and status are valued in a culture, the more formal your presentation and acceptance of business cards should be.

When presenting your business card to an international associate, be certain to present it in the language of your recipient—an English translation should be on the reverse side. Holding the card in both hands as you present it signifies its importance. When receiving your associate's business card, take the time to read it carefully, noting the person's name, title, and other distinguishing characteristics. It's considered rude and disrespectful to accept a card and put it away without reading the information first. Even worse, never jot down a few words on the face of the card which, in the mind of your associate, may be tantamount to defacing it.

D INING ETIQUETTE

While overseas, expect to dine out with business associates on many occasions. When Marshall was in Asia, he sampled such delicacies as pig ears, barbecued ox meat, smoked ox tenderloin, chicken wings with opium poppy seeds, turtle soup, duck feet, and chicken testicles. He also ate raw horse meat—which he claims tastes like pastrami—locusts, whale meat, and dog. (Still have your bags packed?) Remember, your international hosts will be curious to see how you react when sampling these and other sorts of novelties. (Of course, Americans are not the only ones who react with shock to unusual and unfamiliar foods. International visitors to the United States sometimes have similar reactions when asked to sample such all-American favorites as grits, corn-on-the-cob, and watermelon.)

While you will be exposed to many unusual foods overseas, keep in mind that your international hosts may be sensitive to foods that you consider normal. For example, Moslems do not eat pork, and Hindus shun beef because cows are considered sacred in India. The particular rules of dining etiquette vary according to culture. For that reason, it pays to spend time learning culturally appropriate table manners, including how to eat particular foods properly. At the very least, you'll want to know how to use chopsticks well if you're traveling in the Far East. It also makes good business sense to research the etiquette of dinner conversation and whether or not it's appropriate to discuss business over meals. Polish off your knowledge of international dining etiquette by mastering the rules of tipping and making toasts in your host country.

G IFT GIVING

The practice of giving gifts to show appreciation is an acceptable custom in most cultures. When working abroad, you should be prepared to both present and receive gifts with business associates. Yet the type of gift you select, and when and how you present and receive gifts, can be fraught with cultural undertones. Anyone can make a blunder when not up on current gift-giving practices in the host country. Letitia Baldrige, the former chief of staff for Jackie Kennedy, shares an example in her book, *New Complete Guide to Executive Manners*. She tells how she had intended to present several Hindu officials with custom-made cowhide picture frames. Oops. Fortunately, she realized her mistake before presenting the gifts.

I've certainly had my own share of global gift faux pas. For instance, I once complimented an Iranian client on the beautiful white scarf she was wearing. She thanked me, then proceeded to remove the scarf and offer it to me, which was the custom in her culture. We spent several awkward moments during which I attempted to decline her gift and she insisted that I take it. Had I known of the custom in advance, I could have saved us both considerable discomfort and embarrassment. Imagine what might have happened had I enthused over her Jaguar coupe convertible. Hmm . . .

In the Japanese culture, presentation is everything when it comes to giving gifts. With the beautiful Japanese wrapping paper, it's easy to see why. When receiving a gift in Japan, it's customary to offer thanks and then open the gift later, in private. I shudder when I think of how many Japanese guests I unknowingly offended before learning of their custom. I would often rip open their gifts with great gusto and gush my thanks, completely oblivious to the norms.

Unless you take the time to inquire about the gift-giving customs in your host country, you risk making the same type of gaffes that I did. With a little bit of research, though, you can make a positive and memorable impression instead. Select just the right gift for your host, present it appropriately, and score big points for your cultural know-how.

APPROPRIATE DRESS

We North Americans have a tendency to dress down. With the introduction of "casual Fridays" into the workplace, this trend has become even more pronounced. Remember, however, that most of the rest of the world dresses up for business, at least more than what you're probably used to.

Also keep in mind that women traveling and working in Muslim countries are expected to dress modestly. You should wear a jacket or sweater to cover a sleeveless or short-sleeved blouse and wear skirts that cover the knees. In Egypt, I observed what can happen if you don't follow these rules. Against our strong warnings, one of the women in our group decided to venture out wearing shorts and a tank top. We later rescued her from a small group that had gathered around her. They let her know in no uncertain terms that her dress was not acceptable or welcome there. End of story.

LANGUAGE CONCERNS

You don't need to be fluent in a second language to be able to communicate across cultures. However, you *do* need to know what gets in the way of your communicating effectively and what to do about it. Here are some of the comments that international clients share about their difficulty communicating with Americans:

- Americans speak too fast.
- They don't give me enough time to say what I want.
- Their accent is unfamiliar.
- I can't understand their vocabulary.
- Their body language is different from mine.
- Americans are too loud.
- They speak to me like a child.
- They don't speak clearly.
- Their humor is difficult for me to understand.
- Sometimes they seem angry when I can't answer quickly.
- It's hard to understand Americans over the telephone.

It probably won't surprise you to learn that many Americans express similar frustrations when the situation is reversed. Father Wells describes his experience traveling in Cuba: "Berlitz's Spanish-English dictionary gives the word *autobús* as the Spanish equivalent of the English *bus*. Instead, in Cuba, I kept hearing the expression *wawa*, which turns out to be the way they pronounce the word *guagua*. And guagua means bus in parts of Latin America."

EXPECT A FEW MISTAKES

No amount of planning and research will have you acting like a local overnight. Misunderstandings are bound to happen. Here's an example. Arriving in Paris from Switzerland, I decided to treat myself at a café in the shadow of the great cathedral, Notre Dame. I was taking in the local scenery, sipping my glass of Côte du Rhone, and savoring the experience of hearing French spoken faster than the speed of light. Alas, my hopes of blending in inconspicuously among the local patrons were dashed the moment I attempted to pay for my meal. I placed my coins on the table, but the garçon replied, "Non!" and repeated how much I owed. Again, I placed my coins on the table, only to be met this time with a louder version of Non!—until the final crescendo of NON! interrupted conversations all around me. Finally, I dumped all the change I had on the table and let the garçon take what was due. That evening, I told myself that I wouldn't go out in public again until I had learned how to handle my money. My "aha!" came soon afterward, when I realized that some of the francs I had tried to use as payment were Swiss francs, not French ones. That simply would not do in Paris.

Foreign accents may also seem incomprehensible at first. Father Wells continues: "When Marie speaks to me in French, I mostly understand her—but she's speaking carefully and more slowly for my benefit. But when I go to France and haven't been hearing the language for awhile, lots of the words seem to run together, plus people generally are speaking more rapidly."

Indeed it's frustrating when you've learned another language, yet are unable to understand it when it's spoken by native speakers. When you know where the communication problems lie, however, you can begin to do something about them. Here are a few suggestions:

When you're the speaker, slow down your speech somewhat and

When Bill and his family were living abroad, his wife went shopping for groceries not long after they arrived. When the butcher asked her how much meat she wanted, she replied, "Two," thinking she'd asked for two pounds. Instead, she ended up with two kilos of meat, which is about four pounds. Although that mistake wasn't a bad one, Bill would often find his wife in tears after more difficult misunderstandings. Gradually, she became comfortable in the new culture and learned her way around.

Her frustration is a common experience among newly arrived expatriates. How do you shop when you can't read the labels and you don't recognize the produce? An international student once told me that she had never seen an avocado before. She reasoned that it would be safe to eat if she boiled it first, and she did. Mmm . . .

To sum it all up, as Jack advises, "Give the experience a chance. . . . Meet people and do things. The ones who get the most out of living overseas are those who get out and discover the local culture and meet people outside their own nationality." In short, living and working abroad can be one of the greatest experiences of your life, if you go with an open heart—and adequate preparation.

speak clearly. Use common vocabulary words and short, simple sentences. Be careful not to talk down to the other person, however. Whatever you do, avoid speaking loudly to get your point across. If the problem is comprehension, the listener won't be able to understand you any better when you raise your voice. Your listener might even misinterpret your loudness as anger.

Avoid using acronyms, jargon, slang, clichés, idioms, and puns that would cause your listener confusion. Imagine how someone with a limited understanding of English would interpret such phrases as: "You're pulling my leg," "That's it in a nutshell," and "You bet!" Keep in mind that even when people speak a second language well, it's often difficult for them to understand and appreciate foreign humor. They might take your teasing or sarcasm seriously.

Finally, complement your speech with gestures that can fill in missing details in the listener's comprehension. If your listener still doesn't understand, restate the information or question in a different way. Often, the listener may have an idea of what you're saying, but is not completely sure. Restating the information gives both of you the chance to confirm that your meaning is understood.

When you're the listener, give the speaker sufficient time to finish talking before responding. Sometimes, this is easier said than done—but don't get impatient. Your impatience or irritation may discourage or embarrass speakers to the point that they stop trying to communicate with you altogether.

With time, you'll be able to understand more than you thought you could initially. It's important not to stop listening when you hear unfamiliar words or a thick accent. You might have to listen a little longer and in a different way. Yet, if you exercise patience and practice, you'll be surprised at how much headway you can make.

G ESTURES AND BODY LANGUAGE

Using gestures and body language to communicate in another culture is risky. Take the handshake, for example. While it's often used in business greetings and introductions around the world, its meaning is open to interpretation. North Americans tend to prefer a firm handshake, held for two or three seconds. When someone offers us a limp or partial handshake, we jump to all kinds of conclusions. We assume that the person is weak or lacking in self-confidence. Even worse, we may think the person doesn't want to shake hands with us. (Note that in Japan, you may receive a slight bow instead of a handshake. In India, a woman might use the *Namasté* greeting, with the palms of the hands pressed together at chest height, as if in prayer. The gesture translates as "I honor the God within you.")

I once asked a male friend why I often received a weak handshake from men. His response surprised me. He said that many men were probably afraid of hurting me with their grips. If I hadn't asked the question, I wouldn't have understood their intent. When I share this story with North American women in my audience, many of them express dismay. They hasten to assure men that it's OK, even preferable, to offer women firm handshakes. At the same time, if someone shakes hands too vigorously, we're often quick to assume that the person is aggressive and insensitive. If a handshake is subject to misinterpretation in one culture, think about the effect across cultures, especially between men and women in social settings.

People of the same culture share an unspoken understanding of how much physical distance to leave between one another. Generally speaking, mainstream North Americans prefer to have a bubble of at least 18 inches between themselves and another person. If someone moves too far into your personal space, you may feel uncomfortable or even threatened—you might back away from the person. However, if the person entering your space is from the Middle East, he or she may interpret your movement as, well, standoffish. In Middle Eastern culture, it's perfectly appropriate to stand close enough to another person to feel his or her breath on your face.

You can imagine how this cultural difference might play out: The North American takes a step back, and the Middle Easterner moves forward to close the distance between them. This step causes the American to move back again, creating a cultural dance that ends only when the American's back is up against the wall. In the meantime, the people involved in the dance are drawing conclusions about what the other person's movements mean.

There are numerous other gestures that can make or break a cross-cultural interaction. Research and flexibility are your allies in preparing to handle any difficulties that arise because of them.

SMOKING AND DRINKING

Two of the most challenging situations you can face abroad involve smoking and social drinking. As a rule, smoking has declined in public places throughout the United States. This is generally not the case overseas, where smoking is allowed in most places. Unless you're in your own home or your company has a nonsmoking policy (unlikely abroad), you will lack the authority to ask someone to refrain from smoking in your presence.

If you are a nonsmoker, the best you can do to avoid secondhand smoke is position yourself near an open door or window whenever possible. Alternatively, you could move your chair somewhat off to the side if a smoker is sitting near you. If asked, simply explain that you're allergic to smoke or that it irritates your contact lenses (if you wear them).

Drinking might also pose problems for Americans overseas. Marshall quickly learned that social drinking after business hours was the "lubrication of relationships" in Asia. He drank because it was a necessary part of doing business with the Japanese—but he didn't like it. So he learned how to pace his drinking when socializing throughout long evenings and into the wee hours of the morning. He concentrated on his senses. When necessary, he excused himself and took a brief break in the rest room before rejoining the group.

On the other hand, if you're already a social drinker, you might find it difficult to work in Saudi Arabia and other Muslim countries, where drinking alcohol is forbidden. Expatriates who want to drink learn to be quite resourceful in such places, but it's always risky to flout the local laws.

TRANSLATORS AND INTERPRETERS

For the record, translators are people who change *written* words in documents into another language. Interpreters translate *spoken* words into another language. Don't assume that a translator can also act as an interpreter. Though similar, the two professions require different language skills.

Even when handled by highly skilled professionals, translations and interpretations can go awry. Here are a couple of well-known examples: General Motors attempted to market its popular economy car, the Nova, in Latin America. Unfortunately for GM, *nova* means "no go" in Spanish—not exactly an enticement to buy a car. The American movie *Free Willy* was distributed in England under the same title. To the English, *willy* refers to a part of the male anatomy—I'm not sure whether or not this fact hurt movie sales. Finally, former U.S. President George Bush created staggering challenges to his foreign interpreters because he often spoke in incomplete and rambling sentences.

Whether you're the president of a country, the president of an international organization, or anybody else, you'll want to be understood abroad in the way you've intended. If you've hired an interpreter for a business meeting, for example, allow him or her to review meeting materials in advance. During the meeting, give the interpreter enough time to translate your words into the second language. By working closely together, you and the interpreter can do much to eliminate the possibility of misinterpretation and inadvertent offense.

Translating written documents into the language of your host country is not only a matter of courtesy and respect, but it also increases understanding among business partners. For that reason, you'll want to have your business materials handled by an accredited translator. Be certain that he or she is not only fluent but is also *current* in the second language. Otherwise, your translated materials could end up sounding old-fashioned, hopelessly out of date, or just plain wrong. You can locate translators through the American Translators Association in Alexandria, Virginia, 703/683-6100.

S OCIAL CUSTOMS AND SENSITIVITIES

Is it socially acceptable for two females to walk hand-in-hand down the street in a certain culture? What about two males? What are the cultural implications if they do? In a specific country, what are the norms in regard to dating, drinking alcohol, using profanity, self-disclosure, or writing thank-you notes? Questions of social norms can perplex Americans overseas—and it's easy to make mistakes.

I received an education about cultural sensitivities close to home when I was invited to the home of visiting Arab students for dinner. They watched closely as I served myself food, then the conversation stopped. Finally, one of my hosts explained their discomfort: I was using my left hand. In Arab countries, using the left hand for anything but personal hygiene is unacceptable. That makes it difficult when you're left-handed as I am, doesn't it? Yet my objective was to fit in with my hosts' culture, even though we were sharing a meal in the United States. I would have been wise under those circumstances to take their lead and start improving my dexterity.

You'll undoubtedly discover other customs and sensitivities on your own. As with business practices, be sure to research the social customs of your host country before you go abroad.

INTERNATIONAL CORRESPONDENCE

Success in international relationships depends upon face-to-face meetings. Yet it's hard to completely escape using e-mail and fax when you cannot meet in person. Just remember that technology is a supplement to face-to-face communication—not a replacement for it. Technology is also a globalizing force, often transcending cultural boundaries. But when using technology to communicate across cultures, you'll need to be careful and remember differences in language and customs.

When sending e-mail or a faxed letter to foreign colleagues, offer your greetings before jumping into the business at hand. After all, you're trying to build a relationship here. Avoid using uppercase letters, which often give the impression that you're shouting or angry. More than ever, it's important for your sentences to be brief, concise, and positive. Avoid asking yes or no questions, since you could easily misinterpret the responses. Perhaps the most important thing to remember is that e-mail and fax are not private. You can't be sure who will read them. Therefore, don't send any message or material that you wouldn't want someone other than your intended recipient to see.

Needless to say, you will learn countless other language and cultural lessons as you travel, live, and work abroad. My intent is not to make you an expert in cross-cultural encounters but rather to make you aware of potential areas of cultural difference. When you're aware, you can work with host nationals to quickly resolve any misunderstandings or conflicts.

COUNTRY-BY-COUNTRY PROFILES

Before beginning your overseas assignment, research the rules of punctuality, conversation, negotiating, decision making, seating arrangements, and gender roles in your host county. Here are thumbnail sketches of business practices in some of the most popular areas for overseas employment.

All but one of these areas—Saudi Arabia—is either a frequent destination or an emerging destination for companies surveyed by the NFTC in 1998. Because Saudi Arabia employs a large number of U.S. citizens, I've included it as well.

Admittedly, presenting such information involves an inherent risk. Exceptions can always be found, and cultures change, often from one generation to the next. Therefore, use this information only as a general guide to behavior at work and in social situations. Whether you are employed in educational, nonprofit, government, or business work abroad, these cultural guidelines can help you navigate interactions. Remember, though, this brief guide is not meant to replace your own in-depth research.

Australia

Country and Cultural Overview Relaxed, warm, friendly, extremely hospitable—these are just a few of the adjectives that travelers use to describe Australians. Whether the purpose of your journey is to visit, conduct business, or live and work among them, Australians have the ability to make you feel completely at ease from the moment you're introduced.

Unfortunately, Australia has been plagued by high unemployment in the 1990s, making it difficult for foreigners to find work here. However, persistent job seekers may discover opportunities in teaching and technical positions down under.

Business Basics Outsiders may mistake Australian informality and joie de vivre for naiveté in business, but nothing could be further from the truth. Australians by and large are well educated and business savvy. They tend to be direct and take a no-nonsense approach to business matters. They'll appreciate it if you do the same. Leave your pretensions at home and level with them. If you're hoping to impress them with your wealth, education, or influence, you can save your breath. Rank and status will probably mean very little to your Australian counterparts. Bring your business cards, but don't expect a ritualistic exchange as is common in Japan and China.

In Australia, you're expected to make appointments in advance and to be punctual in keeping them. Once you've been introduced and made brief small talk, get down to business quickly. Business dress is conservative, but jackets aren't always worn, particularly during summer.

Courtesies Many Westerners find it easy to connect with Australians because their form of greeting is very similar to ours: a firm handshake, together with an honorific title like Sir or Madam. Once your relationship is established, however, you may find people of your own gender addressing you as "mate." Australians also tend to get on a first-name basis fairly quickly, but wait until you are invited to do so.

Negotiations Australians appreciate a straightforward presentation, with no hype or extraneous information. Your best bet is to present the facts of your proposal and not attempt a hard sell. Honesty and sincerity are valued. Australians will generally be pragmatic and concerned with the bottom line. Decisions must be approved by top management, so expect some delay in response to your proposals.

Business Entertaining Many Australians subscribe to a philosophy of hard work and hard play, and they may invite you to get away from business matters for awhile. Invitations might include anything from sharing a beer at a local pub to attending a barbecue or party to a day of swimming or sailing. Business may be discussed on such outings, but let your host take the lead in bringing it up.

Sensitivities While it's OK to express strong opinions in Australia, be wary of comparing Australia with the United States or Great Britain and avoid such sensitive political areas as Australia's treatment of its Aborigines.

Holidays Australian holidays include:
- January 1—New Year's Day
- January 26—Australia Day
- Good Friday
- Easter
- Easter Monday
- April 25—Anzac Day
- Second Monday in June—Queen's Birthday
- December 25—Christmas
- December 26—Boxing Day

Brazil

Country and Cultural Overview Beautiful Brazil, the largest country in South America, attracts business travelers and tourists alike, despite its volatile economy and social unrest. From its samba beat and passion for soccer to the smells and tastes of its local cuisine, Brazil is a treat for the senses. While business dealings are taken seriously here, the country boasts a warm and fun-loving culture that can diminish at least some of the stress of doing business across cultures. Family is first among Brazilians, often influencing hiring practices and business relationships in general. The best job opportunities here are in agriculture, information technology, aviation, and auto manufacturing.

Business Basics Brazilians value long-term business relationships established first through personal contacts. Your contact, or *despechante* in Portuguese, will be instrumental in making the necessary introductions and paving the way for your doing business. Use your networking contacts or inquire at the U.S. consulate or American Chamber of Commerce in Brazil for assistance in hiring an effective contact.

Expect to take time building relationships before getting down to business in Brazil. Brazilians want to know you as a person first, as a business professional second. You'll be offered coffee in a demitasse cup—with the suggestion that you take at least three spoonfuls of sugar—before meetings and given the chance to make small talk about common interests.

You'll find some disparity in business practices between Rio de Janeiro, where the atmosphere is somewhat relaxed, and Sao Paulo, the center of corporate enterprise. As my Brazilian friends explained: "If you want to work, go to Sao Paulo; if you want to play and have a good time, come to Rio." While appointments will be scheduled in advance, Brazilians in Rio, unlike those in Sao Paulo, have a relaxed view of punctuality and may arrive late for your meeting. This situation might take some getting used to, especially if you have a "Type A personality," but it is the cultural norm. If you're confused as to whether or not you should arrive on time or stylishly late, it's best to err on the side of promptness until you feel comfortable in your relationship. Business dress in Rio also tends to be less formal than in Sao Paulo. Be sure to have your business cards translated into Portuguese, the official language of Brazil, and not Spanish.

Courtesies In Brazil, it's customary to greet all individuals with a handshake, in both business and social settings, upon arrival and when taking your leave. If you have established a close working relationship over time, you may embrace each other; women often touch alternate cheeks and kiss the air. This gesture can be quite disconcerting if you are trying to really kiss, instead of touch, the cheek of your Brazilian counterpart.

Titles such as Doctor, Senhor, and Senhora are commonly used before a person's family name. Note that Brazilian family names, a combination of the mother and father's last names, can be lengthy and confusing to the uninitiated. As a result, titles are often used with the person's first name alone. Despite the use of titles in address, you'll find that Brazilians tend to get on a first-name basis fairly quickly.

Negotiations Brazilians love to bargain, so be prepared for lengthy negotiations spread out over several meetings. Expressive gestures and proximity are part of the Brazilian culture and can often be intimidating to outsiders, particularly when negotiating. The intense, emotional Brazilian communication style may leave you feeling very energized, very tired, or both. Your best strategy is to demonstrate patience, avoid expressing your frustration, and offer a spirited presentation yourself.

Business Entertaining Brazilians entertain in restaurants, private clubs, and, only occasionally, private homes. Unless your host indicates otherwise, your best bet is to arrive a bit later than the suggested time, perhaps by 15 minutes or so. Once you arrive, you can expect talk of business matters to evolve gradually rather than immediately. While it's not necessary to bring a gift for the host when invited to a home, sending flowers the next day will be appreciated (as long as they're not purple, which signifies death). If you're doing the hosting and happen to be staying at a first-rate hotel, suggest your hotel restaurant as the meeting site, or ask your concierge for another recommendation.

Sensitivities Brazilians take pride in their independence and prefer to be known as Brazilians first, Latin Americans second. Their language is Portuguese, so be careful not to refer to them as Hispanics. They're also sensitive to people from the United States who simply refer to themselves as Americans. They'll be quick to remind you that they, too, are Americans. As you might expect, references to politics, including Brazil's relationship with Argentina and the *favelas*, the Brazilian equivalent of our ghettos, are sensitive areas.

Holidays Remember that the seasons in Brazil are reversed from those in the United States, with summer falling between December and February. In addition, note that Brazilians observe the following holidays:
- January 1—New Year's Day
- January 6—Epiphany
- February or March, five days before Ash Wednesday—Carnival (the country comes to a complete standstill)
- March or April—Easter
- April 21—Tiradentes Day
- May 1—May Day
- September 7—Independence Day
- October 2—Our Lady of Aparecida Day
- November 2—All Soul's Day
- November 15—Proclamation Day
- December 25—Christmas Day

China

Country and Cultural Overview Travel to China for both business and pleasure has increased steadily over the last 20 years, despite occasional political disruptions. Yet the country remains an enigma to most Westerners. Traditional treasures like the Great Wall, Forbidden City, and the Ming Tombs in the capital city of Beijing stand alongside the wonders of modern technology. The sheer size of China, its diverse terrain and weather patterns, its billion-plus inhabitants, and its wide-ranging dialects—all can be overwhelming to outsiders. In a country committed to a communist philosophy, its leaders maintain a delicate balancing act between retaining political control and restructuring the economy. One of China's greatest challenges lies in finding a way to reduce air pollution and soil erosion.

Consumer electronics, telecommunications, and toy manufacturing are among China's strongest industries. Job opportunities are most common in the fields of teaching, business, finance, and technology.

Business Basics As in Brazil, it's important to establish contacts before attempting business dealings in China. The American Chamber of Commerce in Beijing and the U.S. Department of Commerce can help put you in touch with such contacts. The Chinese seek long-term business relationships with foreign investors and take time to develop trust and partnerships. They expect patience from their foreign counterparts in return.

Rank and status play a particularly significant role in China, as they do throughout Asia. Therefore, it's important to consider the impact of behavior that might cause the Chinese to "lose face" (lose honor). Embarrassment of any kind, especially in front of colleagues, could jeopardize a person's reputation and social standing—and reflect badly on you. The Chinese respect and defer to senior leadership. It's advisable for you to do the same: Allow senior colleagues to enter a room first, do not interrupt presentations, and listen attentively until a senior colleague invites you to speak. If you're the senior member of a business group, make sure to coach your team in proper etiquette before meetings.

Arriving late for business appointments is considered impolite. Once introduced, you can expect a formal exchange of business cards. Your bilingual business card should be held with both hands and presented with the Chinese side facing your recipient. How you receive a business card from your Chinese host is equally important. Read the information carefully, then put the card in a card case. Do not write on the card.

Before you begin your business discussions, the Chinese will offer you tea as you exchange pleasantries. Here's an excellent opportunity for you to describe your positive impressions of what you've experienced so far in China—art exhibits, cultural events, or visits to historic sites. The Chinese frown on boasting. Rather, they expect your company's accomplishments to speak for themselves. Modesty and reserve, as opposed to loudness and self-promotion, are valued in business relationships.

The typical business day in China runs from eight to five or nine to six, with lunch between noon and two accordingly. Business dress is generally conservative and neutral in color.

Courtesies It's appropriate to shake hands and bow slightly when meeting the Chinese, though you should wait for the Chinese person to extend a hand first. Because titles are an indication of rank and status, use them with last names whenever possible. The order of Chinese names differs from our own and can be confusing at first. The surname, or family name, comes first, followed by the generational name, then the given, or birth, name. Therefore, a woman named Hu Zi Chang would be addressed as Madame Hu.

The Chinese are uncomfortable being touched by people they've just met or don't know well. As always when initiating international relationships, exercise restraint in your body language and use of gestures.

Negotiations The Chinese are patient and pragmatic in their business dealings, but show little tolerance for ineptitude or lack of preparation from their negotiating counterparts. Knowing that time is money to most North Americans, the Chinese might use your impatience to their advantage when it comes to negotiations. They will be in no hurry to settle the details of your contractual relationship, despite your deadlines. They may even go back to the drawing board when you thought you had reached an acceptable agreement. Nothing is certain in negotiating in China until the final papers are signed. The Chinese are adept negotiators, so do your homework thoroughly before entering into your business discussions.

Business Entertaining Lunches and evening banquets are the primary forms of business entertainment in China. To make the most of your banquet experience, pace your food intake throughout the evening to enjoy the many courses that will be served. Practice using chopsticks ahead of time so that you will have some comfort in using them in front of your Chinese hosts. The Chinese are big on toasting, so come prepared with a suitable toast of your own.

After you've attended a banquet, you'll want to reciprocate with an invitation of your own. Your costs for the event should not exceed the cost of the banquet you previously attended.

Sensitivities Be aware that the Chinese are sensitive to comments from foreigners about human rights issues within the country, the Tiananmen Square uprising, China's relationship with Taiwan, and political leadership.

Holidays Chinese holidays include:
  • January 1—New Year's Day

- Late January or early February—Chinese New Year
- March 8—International Working Women's Day
- May 1—Labor Day
- May 4—Youth Day
- June 1—Children's Day
- July 1—Founding of the Communist Party of China
- August 1—People's Liberation Army Day
- October 1 and 2—National Day

Germany

Country and Cultural Overview At the heart of the European Economic Community lies the Federal Republic of Germany. While it is a major world economic player, Germany is now battling high unemployment and the costs of rebuilding infrastructure in its eastern half. While it can be difficult for foreigners to locate viable work opportunities here, recent advertised positions indicate the need for software engineers and manufacturing sales professionals. English is widely spoken, but if you speak German, you'll increase your odds of both obtaining work and succeeding once employed.

Business Basics Working and doing business in Germany involves an amazing amount of bureaucratic red tape. Rules and regulations must be followed precisely, a situation that can impact project deadlines, productivity, and employee initiative. For many German people, though, regulations provide welcome structure, stability, and discipline. Often, a personal contact—either a colleague or hired assistant—can help you wade through the maze of paperwork and ensure that you've dotted your i's and crossed your t's. One of the best places for making business contacts in Germany is at trade fairs.

Business is taken seriously here, and punctuality at the workplace and business appointments is important. More than likely, you'll find Germans to be formal and reserved in their interactions. Expect minimal small talk before getting down to the business at hand. Formal, conservative dress is standard business attire.

Courtesies The German people shake hands firmly when introduced and upon departure. Traditionally, men do not extend their hands to a woman unless she extends hers first. However, this custom is changing as more women enter the German workforce. When shaking hands, use the person's last name, plus a professional or honorary title.

Negotiations As you might expect, your German hosts will value very detailed and factual information, presented systematically. The final decision on whether or not to accept your proposal will take time. Your German counterparts will want to review the accuracy of your information and reach consensus among themselves.

Business Entertaining It is rare to be invited to the home of a German counterpart unless you have established a friendly relationship. Germans do not tend to integrate business and social relationships, and many live and socialize far from their jobs. Business lunches and dinners at restaurants are relatively common, however.

Sensitivities Avoid personal questions and references to World War II, but be prepared to discuss international events and politics with your German hosts. Sports and cultural activities are also good topics of conversation.

Holidays Public holidays in Germany include:
*   January 1—New Year's Day
*   Good Friday
*   Easter Monday
*   May 1—Labor Day
*   October 3—National Holiday
*   Mid-November—Prayer and Repentance Day
*   December 25—Christmas

India
Country and Cultural Overview India is a country steeped in tradition and rich in its diversity of ethnic groups, languages, and religions. It also lies poised to usurp China, by the year 2025, as the most populated country on the planet. Surrounded by such alluring places as the Arabian Sea and the Bay of Bengal, India evokes an exotic mystique of times past. Yet trade and investment reforms since the early 1990s have propelled India into the spotlight of business development. The government remains

committed to increasing the role of private enterprise and promoting a global economy.

Important industries include agricultural development, high technology, textiles, steel, transportation equipment, mining, petroleum, machinery, and tourism. Most job opportunities are found in the nonprofit sector and in technical fields.

Business Basics   Many Indian people place a strong emphasis on spiritual attainment rather than material goods and are generally fatalistic in their philosophical outlook. That is, they may see no compelling reason to worry about the passing of time or one's lot in life. Such passivity and the importance of social harmony over the needs of the individual often influence how business is conducted.

Courtesies   Titles are as important to the Indian people as they are to most Asians. It's a matter of courtesy and respect to include a person's title in introductions and greetings while avoiding the use of first names. While handshakes are common among men in business settings, they will instead use the traditional gesture known as *Namasté* when greeting women. This greeting is performed by bringing the palms of one's hands together under the chin, as if in prayer, and bowing slightly.

Negotiations   To maintain harmonious relations, business decisions in India often pass through several layers of management. Everyone is able to give input until a consensus is reached. For this reason, it will be in your best interest to present your business proposal to the highest level of management at the first opportunity. Naturally, when many people are involved in making a decision, you can expect the negotiations to take time. Your proposal will be best received when it is well supported by facts, statistical evidence, and the offer of implementation assistance.

Business Entertaining   Business entertaining is often conducted at lunch in India, in hotels or restaurants. Remember that devout Hindus believe that cows are sacred, and therefore don't eat beef, while strict Moslems refrain from eating pork or drinking alcoholic beverages.

To Moslems, the left hand is used for personal hygiene and is considered unclean for use in eating and, to some, even passing or receiving food.

Sensitivities Indian people are sensitive to comments about their recent testing of the nuclear bomb, strained relations with neighboring Pakistan, poverty, and internal ethnic unrest.

Since many Indian people take religion very seriously, avoid making critical comments about its influence on society or specific religious practices.

Holidays National holidays in India include:
- January 1—International New Year's Day
- January 26—Republic Day
- August 15—Independence Day
- October 2—Mohandas Gandhi's birthday

Japan

Country and Cultural Overview Japan has captivated and con- founded the hearts and minds of foreigners from the early days of the shogun. Despite its homogenous population, Japan has a culture that is as intricate as its origami. One folded wing of Japan's social fabric conceals layers of hidden complexities. Herein lies the paradoxical charm and appeal of Japan for many. What you find on the surface is probably not what you will find underneath.

Japan reveres the arts; its most illustrious craftspeople and artisans are designated as living "National Treasures." One path to understanding the Japanese character is to participate in the arts and attend cultural events. Soak up all you can of Kabuki and Noh theater, ikebana, the art of flower arranging, calligraphy, and such martial arts as sumo wrestling and judo.

Japan is still faltering from the effects of its recent deep recession, but it remains among the most technologically advanced nations in the world. Its major markets include pharmaceuticals, motor vehicles and parts, electronic and telecommunication services, machine tools, automated production systems, medical equipment, and fish products. The best job opportunities for U.S. citizens seeking work here are in education, particularly teaching English.

SAFETY AND SECURITY

A number of incidents in recent years have alerted U.S. citizens to the potential dangers of traveling and living abroad. The bombing of the U.S. embassy in Nairobi and the killing of tourists in Luxor, Egypt, are but two of several anti-American incidents that have drawn worldwide attention—and scared American travelers.

Unfortunately, tragic events like these do happen, and they are not easy to predict. Rather than abandoning your dream of traveling, living, and working overseas out of fear, though, learn what you can do to protect yourself.

Start by gathering information. The U.S. State Department issues warnings for specific countries whenever it believes that the safety and security of U.S. citizens traveling there are at risk. What constitutes a risk to Americans overseas? Terrorist attacks, natural catastrophes, and political strife are among the reasons for warning travelers. Currently, the State Department recommends that Americans avoid travel to 28 countries.

At the State Department's Web site (http://travel .state.gov), you can also find Consular Information Sheets that provide detailed country-by-country information of interest to travelers. You'll find information about each country's entry requirements, crime rate, health conditions, medical facilities, traffic safety, and security concerns. Public announcements at the same Web site alert travelers to anniversary dates of previous unrest or terrorism and other short-term threats.

Business Basics Personal connections are essential for doing business in Japan. Your Japanese contact can vouch for you and give you credibility by describing your character, educational background, and company.

The Japanese place great value on ritual and ceremony. In business, rituals include the formal exchange of everything from greetings to

Once you're armed with current information, take steps to make yourself a less visible target overseas. In his riveting book *The Gift of Fear*, author Gavin De Becker says that the most important thing you can do to protect your personal safety is to develop your "intuition for danger." De Becker believes that we should honor, not discount, our instincts.

Residents of large cities like New York develop street smarts at an early age. They learn the art of observing their surroundings without being obvious. You can learn this art, too, and use it to your advantage. As soon as possible when you arrive overseas, get to know your neighbors and mingle with the local population. This is where your friendliness and knowledge of the local language will pay off. But while it's important to be friendly, don't be naive. Be aware of your surroundings and any changing situations, including unfamiliar people or cars. By all means, protect your home and your car. Use security alarms and get a dog whose bark will scare off criminals. Avoid areas where demonstrators or other large groups are congregating. When you're out walking, do so purposefully and wear a money belt. If you're involved in a high-profile business, vary your routine to make it difficult for someone to learn your exact schedule.

Of course, these tips are useful no matter where you live. While traveling and living abroad, however, you are treading in unfamiliar territory—at least initially. You might feel vulnerable abroad in a different way than you would at home. Once you have taken steps to address your safety and security, though, you will undoubtedly feel more at ease in your new location.

business cards to gifts. Preserving the harmony of the group and avoiding behavior that would cause a "loss of face" are standard practices. Loudness and brash behavior are considered impolite and won't win you either respect or friends among the Japanese. Expect punctuality in regard to appointments and wear conservative business attire.

Courtesies Handshakes accompanied by a slight bow are common in business greetings. Expect minimal or indirect eye contact, which is a sign of respect to the Japanese (but often misunderstood as disrespect among Westerners). The most appropriate way to greet your Japanese counterparts is to use their last names plus *san*, which is the same as Mr. or Mrs.

Negotiations Many businesspeople who have negotiated with the Japanese remark on their inscrutability. Indeed, it's important to pay close attention to the subtleties and nuances of your Japanese business associates to be certain that you understand their intended meaning. Present your own information clearly and avoid speaking too much. Get comfortable with silence.

If you don't receive any questions or if the Japanese negotiator says "That would be difficult," it's likely that your negotiations are not going well. Remember that business decisions in Japan require consensus and will take time. But once you receive a positive response, the Japanese will move quickly to implement a decision and will expect you to do the same.

Business Entertaining Business entertaining in Japan generally takes place over dinner in a restaurant, followed by a visit to a karaoke bar, where you will be expected to join in the drinking and singing. After work, entertaining is more than a social event—it's an important means of establishing a business relationship. While the evening can last into the wee hours, you will be expected back at work the next morning, ready to perform your responsibilities. Interestingly, this tradition is one area of Japanese culture that's in flux, as many younger Japanese people are choosing to spend more time with their families after work instead of doing the nightly bar circuit.

Sensitivities Avoid discussing politics and religion in your conversations with Japanese associates.

Holidays When a national holiday falls on Sunday in Japan, the next day (Monday) becomes the holiday. Japanese holidays include:
- January 1—New Year's Day
- January 15—Adult's Day

- February 11—National Founding Day
- March 20 or 21—Vernal Equinox Day
- April 29—Greenery Day
- May 3—Constitution Memorial Day
- May 4—National People's Day
- May 5—Children's Day
- July 20—Marine Day
- September 15—Respect for the Aged Day
- September 23 or 24—Autumn Equinox Day
- October 10—Sports Day
- November 3—Culture Day
- November 23—Labor Thanksgiving Day
- December 23—Emperor's Birthday

Mexico

Country and Cultural Overview Located between the United States to the north and Guatemala to the south, Mexico enjoys both a tropical and a desert climate within its borders. The Mexican people are warm and hospitable hosts who are proud of their Indian and Spanish heritage. They also take pride in their independence and differentiation from the United States and the rest of Latin America, despite sharing Spanish as a common language with all Latin American countries except Brazil. Mexicans are strongly devoted to their families and country and express their feelings for each openly. As an outsider, it may take you time to develop their trust and respect as an equal business partner.

Industries of note in Mexico include iron and steel, petroleum, mining, textiles, clothing, motor vehicles, consumer goods, and tourism. Most job opportunities are found in the nonprofit sector, business, and finance.

Business Basics Mexicans enjoy a friendly, easygoing lifestyle that permeates their business culture. But although your Mexican host may arrive late for business appointments, you should arrive on time. Your hosts will value you as a person, not only as a business associate, and will want to know what you think of their country. With that in mind, plan on taking in the local sites and participating in cultural events regularly. If you're not residing in Mexico, arrive for a business trip early, so you can do a little touring first.

Personal connections are once again the norm for doing business here. It's especially helpful to be referred by a family member or close acquaintance of the person with whom you want to work. Note that Mexicans hold a person's dignity in great regard. Any behavior that could be viewed as a personal or cultural slight, such as derogatory comments about the local cuisine or traffic problems, can quickly end a relationship.

Courtesies Titles are very important to Mexicans. When addressing an individual, use his or her title together with the surname. Note that the surname includes both the father's name, which comes first, and then the mother's name. As you develop a relationship with a Mexican colleague, you may shorten your greeting to the person's title only. First names are used only after your Mexican host has extended the invitation to do so.

Upon introduction and departure, handshakes are common. However, note that you're likely to receive a hug after the second or third meeting. Also, don't be surprised to find Mexican associates touching your arm or shoulder while speaking to you. Mexicans are very comfortable with physical closeness and may misunderstand your reluctance to reciprocate.

Negotiations Mexican executives are often indirect in their negotiating approach. Consequently, as you negotiate, it's important to ask open-ended questions, rather than ones requiring a simple yes or no response. You'll also want to use negotiating and business tactics that complement the norms of this status-conscious country. For example, stay in a first-class hotel and wear tailored business attire that presents the image of a successful executive. Include a high-ranking manager on your team during your presentation and use first-rate visuals to support your proposals. Expect some interruptions and delays in your business discussions, and be sure to control your frustration and impatience. If you don't, your attitude could seriously impede your chances for ultimate success.

Business Entertaining Business discussions in Mexico can take place during breakfast (8 to 8:30 a.m.) or lunch (2 to 4 p.m.), though not before the exchange of preliminary pleasantries. You may be invited to dinner, which is usually served after 8:30 p.m., but this is not an appropriate time for business discussions. If you are invited to an individual's home, it's customary to bring flowers as a gift.

Sensitivities Many Mexicans are sensitive about people from the United States referring to themselves simply as Americans. After all, Latin Americans are also Americans. Unfavorable comparisons between Mexico and other Latin American countries or Mexico and the United States are also sensitive areas and best avoided.

Holidays Public holidays in Mexico include:
- January 1—New Year's Day
- March 21—Benito Juárez's birthday
- May 1—Labor Day
- May 5—Cinco de Mayo
- September 16—Independence Day
- October 12—Columbus Day
- November 20—Revolution Day
- December 12—Day of the Virgin Guadalupe
- December 25—Christmas

Saudi Arabia

Country and Cultural Overview In the 1930s, Saudi Arabia won what amounted to the international lottery with its unexpected discovery of oil. Almost overnight, this relatively unknown and undeveloped nation burst onto the world economic scene and underwent exponential growth. In a country whose primary revenue had come from the export of dates and from religious pilgrimages to its holy city of Makkah (Mecca), the shock must have been overwhelming. Today the country offers a fascinating juxtaposition between time-honored traditions based on the teachings of Islam and the fruits of a thriving commercial economy.

Saudi Arabia employs an estimated 4 million foreign workers in the oil, health care, and service industries. Because foreigners tend to live in segregated communities, you may have minimal interaction with Saudis. Nevertheless, you'll need to know about cultural norms when living and doing business in the country. Generally, you'll find the Saudi people to be warm and hospitable hosts who can be intense and emotional in their interactions. Proximity in business and social situations is valued, and you may find yourself standing uncomfortably close to your Saudi hosts.

Business Basics Business practices are based on the teachings and values of Islam, the only legal religion in Saudi Arabia. Indeed Islam is more than a religion here—its threads are woven into every aspect of the nation's cultural fabric. It is the foundation of all interactions and decisions. For example, women and men serve very different and segregated functions in society, and few women are permitted in business roles. Family members come first in business transactions, as well as in personal life.

Here again, you'll need personal and professional connections to do business. You cannot enter Saudi Arabia without a sponsor, who will be able to make introductions and appointments for you. If you don't have a personal connection, contact your state Trade Department for assistance. Naturally, the better connected and more influential your sponsor, the greater the likelihood that you'll succeed. If you're employed by an organization such as Aramco, the company will act as your sponsor.

The workweek in Saudi Arabia runs from Saturday through Wednesday. Friday is the Islamic day of worship. During the holy month of Ramadan, companies usually keep abbreviated business hours.

Punctuality is the cultural norm for guests, though your Saudi host may arrive a few minutes later than the appointed time. Business dress is conservative. Women should dress modestly.

Courtesies While shaking hands during introductions is common, you may also receive a traditional greeting from Saudis—kisses exchanged on both cheeks. This gesture is not common in business situations unless the parties have some familiarity with each other, however. Address your Saudi host by title and first name, not family name.

It's polite to accept your host's offer of coffee or tea and to exchange pleasantries about shared interests. In fact, engaging in extended small talk is a prerequisite to doing business here. Saudis want to get to know your character before getting down to business.

Negotiations Negotiating with the Saudis requires stamina, courtesy, and goodwill. Maintain steady eye contact while you present your proposal. Saudis have a reputation for being hard negotiators, so be well prepared with your information.

Business Entertaining Chances are you'll be invited to the home of your host for dinner. Be prepared to remove your shoes at the door. Remember that alcohol and pork are forbidden and that eating or passing food with your left hand is considered offensive.

Sensitivities Take care to avoid behavior that may be viewed as an insult to the Saudi's religious beliefs, family, or personal honor. For example, sitting with legs crossed, with the sole of your foot showing to your host, is considered an offensive gesture. Discussions of religion and politics are best avoided. Focus instead on such topics as sports, local sites of interest, and popular regional foods.

Holidays Holiday dates vary from year to year because the Islamic calendar is based on the lunar month. The one holiday that doesn't vary is National Day, September 23. The most significant Islamic holidays include Eid al-Fitr at the end of Ramadan, Eid al-Adha (the Feast of the Sacrifice), and the birthday of the Prophet Mohammed.

Singapore

Country and Cultural Overview The island of Singapore, located between Malaysia and Indonesia, is one of the most Westernized nations in Asia. The population is mainly Chinese (the dominant culture), Malay, and Indian. Malay, Mandarin, and Tamil, in addition to English, are spoken by the local population.

Mike, a former Hong Kong expatriate, describes his visit to Singapore as like "a trip to Disneyland. The sun always shines, people always smile." Well, maybe not exactly, but Singapore's residents do live in an exceptionally safe and clean (some would say antiseptic) environment. When you add the fact that English is the language of choice in business, government, and law, it's easy to see why people from the United States often adapt well and quickly to living here. English creates a level playing field for outsiders doing business across Singapore's great diversity of cultures.

Note that the nation's safety and cleanliness can exact a high price.

Singapore enforces strict laws that forbid a number of practices that are common elsewhere. For example, it's illegal to chew gum, litter, spit, jaywalk, and smoke in public places unless so designated. Breaking any of these laws, by either residents or visitors, can result in stiff penalties and fines. Punishment is far worse if you're found with illegal drugs, pornographic materials, or firearms. Nevertheless, many residents feel that the limits on their freedoms are well worth the social benefits they get in return.

Concrete and steel skyscrapers that dot the locale are evidence of the country's rise in economic power. Though this power has been tempered of late because of the worldwide financial crisis, the island continues to attract foreign investors. The largest industries with potential job opportunities for foreigners are manufacturing, commerce, construction, financial and business services, transportation, and communications.

Business Basics A strong sense of family pervades Singapore's culture, and nepotism is a well-honored business tradition. If you have family contacts who can introduce you to company executives, so much the better. A polite demeanor will also serve you well here. As in many Asian countries, deference is given to age and seniority, and any action that would cause your host to "lose face" is a serious transgression. The ritualistic exchange of bilingual business cards is standard practice here, as it is in China and Japan. Don't be surprised or put off by what you might consider inappropriate smiling or laughing from your host. This behavior often indicates nervousness or embarrassment rather than amusement.

Singapore's high heat and humidity dictate a more casual business dress than you'll find in many other Asian countries. Men might not wear jackets or ties, but you'll want to have them in your wardrobe to make a positive first impression.

Courtesies A handshake accompanied by a small bow is the most common form of greeting among business professionals in Singapore. You may encounter different gestures from less Westernized Singaporeans, particularly women, who may not feel comfortable extending their hands. It's always wise to let the local inhabitants take the lead here. The same rules for addressing people apply in Singapore as in China—it's polite to use a person's title along with his or her family name. For example, Doctor Lau Li

Peng would be called Doctor Lau. If he doesn't have a professional title, Mr. Lau is the appropriate greeting.

Standing close or touching another person will be unwelcome and create discomfort. If you are introduced to small children, refrain from patting them on the head, which is considered sacred by many Indian and Malay people.

Negotiations You'll gain respect in your business negotiations by exhibiting calm, patience, and a quiet manner while presenting proposals. An aggressive approach will cause you to lose the trust and respect of your potential business partners. Among Singaporeans, group consensus is valued in reaching final business decisions.

Business Entertaining Attending social events with your Singaporean host is a wonderful way to build rapport and absorb the local culture. Business matters may be discussed over meals, though not usually at someone's home. If you are invited to someone's home, a small gift of candy or flowers will be appreciated. When dining with Malays or Indian people, don't be surprised to see them eat with their right hands. Remember, the left hand is used only for personal hygiene among Moslems.

Sensitivities Note that Singaporeans are sensitive to remarks about their laws, religions, and politics.

Holidays Public holidays in Singapore represent the diversity of ethnic groups and religions that exist here. Note that some holidays have variable dates, so you'll need to check on specific dates by year. The recognized public holidays in Singapore include:
- January 1—International New Year's Day
- January–February—Taipusam, Hindu celebration
- February 1—Federal Day
- March—Prophet Mohammed's birthday (date varies)
- May 1—Labor Day
- May–June—Vesak Day (celebrating the birth, enlightenment, and death of Buddha)

- June—Dayak, end of rice harvest (date varies)
- August 9—National Holiday
- October–November—Deepavali (celebrates Lord Rama's slaying of the mythical tyrant Ravana)
- December 25—Christmas
- Hari Raya Haji (date varies; a holiday of significance to those who have completed the pilgrimage to Mecca)

United Kingdom

Country and Cultural Overview The United Kingdom is located in the British Isles and includes Northern Ireland, Scotland, Wales, and England. (For the record, Great Britain includes only England, Scotland, and Wales). The recently completed Chunnel, the tunnel that connects England and France under the English Channel, is the jewel in the crown of England's technological achievement.

While other members of the European Union have embraced the new Euro currency, England has chosen to retain its independence—at least for the time being. The capital city of London is recognized as one of the world's great trade and financial centers. Most job opportunities in the United Kingdom (and the European community) are found in the business, finance, and technical fields. Growing industries include machinery production, electronics and communications equipment, petroleum, paper products, food processing, textiles, clothing, and other consumer goods.

Business Basics The countries of the United Kingdom share English as a common language, though Welsh and Scottish are sometimes spoken. While accepted business practices vary somewhat among the countries, a traditional, conservative approach is generally the norm. You can expect directness, to the point of bluntness, from your British counterparts. Punctuality at meetings and appointments and business formality, in both dress and discussions, are respected.

Courtesies Handshakes are customary among men in business settings; women may not always extend their hands. It won't take long to get on a first-name basis with your British counterparts. However, as always in international business dealings, wait until your host has invited you to do so. When introduced, both parties usually extend the greeting, "How do you do?" This is a rhetorical question and not meant to be answered with "Fine, thank you." The British use honorary titles ("Mr. Weatherhead") rather than business titles ("Director Weatherhead").

Negotiations Business decisions are considered and deliberate, which can lengthen the negotiating process. Americans have a reputation in the United Kingdom for being overly demonstrative and emotional. You'll receive greater respect and appreciation if you tone down your enthusiasm and stick to the facts. Present well-structured and detailed information in your proposals. Avoid hype and self-promotion and let the facts speak for themselves.

Business Entertaining Business entertaining often takes place at lunch or dinner, in restaurants and private homes. Breakfast meetings are much less common than they are in the United States. Your hosts will appreciate a gift of flowers or candy when you visit them at home. Following dinner, you may be invited to attend a social or cultural event. It's appropriate to reciprocate by inviting your host to lunch or dinner afterward.

Sensitivities The British people view themselves as distinct from other Europeans. Generally speaking, people from England prefer to be referred to as British rather than English. Those living in Scotland, Wales, and Northern Ireland most certainly do not want to be called English.

The British are uncomfortable with too much self-disclosure and with personal questions. Avoid jokes about the royal family and questions about politics, especially relations between England and Northern Ireland.

Holidays Holidays in the United Kingdom include:
- January 1—New Year's Day
- Good Friday
- Easter Monday
- First Monday in May—May Day
- Last Monday in May—Spring Bank Holiday
- Last Monday in August—Summer Bank Holiday

- December 25—Christmas
- December 26—Boxing Day

WHAT WILL YOU DO NEXT

Before continuing to the next chapter, take these steps to reach your dream of living and working abroad:

- Brush up on the customs and language of the country where you intend to live and work.
- Interview nationals for a perspective on what to expect when living and working in their country.
- Attend local art and cultural events to gain a greater understanding of the host country.

9

Get Readjusted— Welcome Home!

So nothing is as sweet as a man's own country, his own parents, even though he's settled down in some luxurious house, off in a foreign land and far from those who bore him.

The Odyssey

After successfully completing your work assignment abroad, you'll need to prepare yourself psychologically and logistically for your journey home. This isn't always easy. "I still have the repatriation blues," says Bill, "and I've been back three years.... My daughter still asks, and she's in college, 'Daddy, when are we going back?'" In this chapter, you'll discover how to make the transition home easier.

WHAT'S SO HARD ABOUT GETTING BACK TO WHERE YOU ONCE BELONGED?

On my bookshelf, I have two books shelved next to each other. One is *You Can't Go Home Again* by Thomas Wolfe. The other is *You Can Go Home Again* by Nora Johnson. The titles remind me of the conflicting messages that expatriates receive about returning home after their international assignments—that feeling of being betwixt and between, neither here nor there. Which feeling will it be for you when it comes to returning home after working abroad? Can you or can't you make a successful transition?

Well, unless you've done something *really* bad while based abroad— something that's landed you in a foreign prison someplace—you *can* go home again. At least in the literal sense, you can. But you won't be the same person coming home that you were when you left for your international assignment. As a result, for many expatriates, the most difficult part about working globally is coming home. The longer you've been away, the longer it can take you to adjust to being back in your own country. Just as jet lag is a real affliction, whether your flight is coming or going, "reverse culture shock" is a real aftereffect of returning home.

You may have undergone profound, life-changing experiences, even during a short assignment abroad. But when you come home, you might find that your friends' lives have gone on pretty much the same as before. Not only that, your friends won't necessarily be as interested in hearing about your adventures abroad as you would like them to be. Even when they want to listen to your stories, they might not have any cultural reference points by which to understand and appreciate what you've gone through. Returning military veterans who have faced danger abroad report similar experiences. They are often met with either indifference or complete incomprehension at home when they try to explain their profound experiences overseas.

Your experience of reverse culture shock might be heightened by changes that *have* taken place at home in your absence. Perhaps your friends have moved or gone on to new jobs, even different relationships. Perhaps your city itself has changed. Reading about the changes in a newspaper or hearing about them from friends is one thing. It's quite another to experience those changes firsthand. As Bill explains: "I was born and raised in New York City, and what I saw when I came back wasn't the slow deterioration, but everything all at once. [The risk of going global is that] you lose touch with what's going on in your environment. I felt like a foreigner in my own country." In Bill's case, a number of events contributed to his reverse culture shock. Consequently, he left his parent company soon after his return home. Even now, Bill misses the international experience so much that he doesn't want to travel abroad—it makes him too nostalgic.

Cultural differences can present other obstacles. For example, Gail found it difficult to readjust to the pace of life in the United States after living in Europe. She realized how fast-paced and stressed out many Americans were. Europeans, in her experience, seemed more family-oriented and more successful in living a balanced life.

It might also be hard to come home if you received a higher salary and greater benefits while working overseas than you did in the United States. Perhaps your salary allowed you to live a more upscale lifestyle than you were normally used to. You might have enjoyed luxuries like a live-in maid or housekeeper, a transportation allowance, or a housing allowance. The benefits you received were not only financial but also emotional—you acquired a certain level of comfort that comes with a high salary. For Gail, who worked and traveled throughout Europe tax free during her overseas employment, "income shock" was the most difficult aspect of her transition home. As the song goes: How will you keep them down on the farm after they've seen Paree? How indeed?

Along with the financial perks you received, you might have enjoyed a high level of independence and increased responsibilities in your international assignment. You might feel doubtful about finding the same kind of position at home. Bill's fear of just such a scenario came true when, after traveling and living around the world for 10 years, he was offered a position managing a department in South Dakota. If Bill accepted the assignment, he would miss the level of responsibility and independence he'd experienced abroad. He would also miss the cultural components inherent in an international lifestyle. Had his company realized the challenges Bill and his family would face coming home to such an assignment, it might have offered him some alternative relocation options.

Many expatriates find themselves passed over for promotions after returning home, usually because they've been out of the organizational mainstream. Some employees return home to find that their former positions are now occupied by someone else or have been eliminated altogether.

People sometimes need to return home early from international assignments. Often, they return because they must care for aging parents. Others are sent home earlier than expected because their organization's business needs change or because the local economy has failed. It's hard enough to come home at the planned time. Even under the best of circumstances, relocation is stressful, if for no other reason than managing the logistics of moving. But when your return is driven by circumstances outside of your control, your experience of reverse culture shock can be that much more severe. Add your family's culture shock to your own, and you have the potential for rough waters ahead.

Considering these examples of reverse culture shock, is it any wonder that one recent survey found that as much as 25 percent of expatriates leave their companies within two years of returning home? Expatriates I interviewed give varied reasons for their departures. Yet the majority of them expressed their frustration at not feeling valued or being given the chance to use their newly developed skills back at home.

Despite the difficulties of coming back home after traveling, living, and working abroad, you can minimize reverse culture shock. With adequate preparation, coming home can be every bit as much of an adventure as going overseas was in the beginning. Let's look at some of the ways you can make it easier to get back to where you once belonged.

R EENTERING THE DOMESTIC JOB MARKET

As Walter Cronkite told a member of his audience who asked how to break into journalism, "Get a job." Ideally, you would have thought about your work upon returning home before ever accepting an international assignment—*ideally*. Of course, reality is often somewhat different from the ideal, as expatriate Mike knows all too well after his two-year assignment in Hong Kong. He explains that he was so excited and busy taking care of logistics that it was hard to devote any energy to planning for his work upon return. "In the beginning, all of your attention is focused on getting to your new posting," he says.

No matter how focused you are on the overseas assignment itself, you need to keep your return in mind. As always when planning your strategy, start by asking questions. In this case: "What do I want to do when I have completed my international assignment?" Answering this question will help you decide how to answer the next two questions: "Where do I want to live next?" and "What type of company or organization do I want to work for?" Let these questions guide you as you begin your transition to employment back home.

Research the Market

Ideally, you've been keeping somewhat abreast of new developments at home while you've been away. Perhaps family members and friends have sent you periodic news clippings about changes in your hometown. Maybe you even kept subscriptions to your local newspapers. Keeping on top of news from home is a good way to prevent reverse culture shock. For instance, higher housing prices and business closings won't surprise you.

If you haven't been keeping up with news from home, now is the time to get serious. Read the paper for information to help in your return. The employment ads will give you some idea about available jobs and hiring trends. But don't stop there. Read between the lines, just as you did when looking for work abroad, to see what hidden work opportunities you might explore. Use the Internet and additional resources that can help you track global job openings.

Network Like Crazy

Sound familiar? It should. We've already discussed networking as a way to increase your chances for overseas success. Guess what? Networking is just as important and effective when you're making plans to return home. Here's how Mike sees it:

> I recommend that you think long and hard about what you want to do after your reentry into your home country. Economic conditions and companies change, but you will not be the same person either when you return.... You need to think about how happy you'll be if you end up back in the job you left behind. Try to think in advance about where your new skills would be most useful and where you'd be challenged by and interested in your work. Make contacts and cement relationships with those business units in advance of your overseas posting if you can.

Start with Company Insiders

If you've stayed in touch with people inside your company at home, they can fill you in on organizational changes in your absence and their impact on employees. You can find out about employee turnover that could have an influence on your position once you return home. Your contacts can also help keep your name alive and your presence felt inside the company, even when you're halfway around the world. New hires will at least hear status reports about your whereabouts and accomplishments, which will make it easier for them to welcome you back to the workforce.

Elena knew it was up to her to find a new position within her company at the end of her assignment in Paris. That's why she started looking actively while still abroad. She also came back for frequent company visits while overseas and kept in touch with lots of people she knew there. Consequently, her transition into a new position at home was relatively painless, and she stayed with the company for another five years.

Check in with Search Consultants

You can begin to explore the job market on the home front, confidentially, through search consultants. Ideally, you've stayed in contact with consultants you spoke with before you left. Like your company leaders, search consultants need to be reminded of the new skills you've gained and accomplishments you've made while working internationally. Keep them posted through quarterly updates, so you won't have to start from scratch in renewing your relationships.

Search consultants can tell you about your prospects for finding the kind of work you want back home and can keep on the alert for positions that might interest you. They can also advise you on how to tailor your resume and highlight your global experience for greater marketability with domestic employers.

Market Yourself

In addition to using company insiders to champion your cause, use other methods to make sure that your company values you as an employee and values your position abroad. You might continue to write articles for your company newsletter and trade publications to increase your visibility. Maintain contact with "the mother ship" with quarterly reports from your international site. Emphasize not only what your team is doing but also the concrete results you've achieved for the company. E-mail your contributions to staff meetings and correspond regularly with other company personnel.

Networking works. There's a reason why people spend considerable time and energy cultivating their business contacts and building relationships. Use the networking skills and contacts you've already developed to overcome the hurdles you face in getting back home and doing work you love.

Ask for Assistance

Whether you're the "trailing spouse" or the international employee, your hiring organization most likely has resources available to help pave the way for your transition home. Even if you didn't negotiate this benefit in your original overseas contract, there's no reason you can't ask for assistance now. Such assistance can include job and family counseling, scouting trips home for both work and housing arrangements, and financial compensation while you're reacclimating to the domestic workforce.

By all means, speak with your mentors for advice about making your next employment move. Just as mentors can guide you in securing work abroad, they can also help in your return. They can keep you posted on job leads, and they can tell you what it's like to return to work at home after an international assignment.

Update Your Resume

Talk with insiders in your company, search consultants, and others in your personal network to learn how best to update your resume. Be sure to highlight your newly acquired international skills. After working globally, you've learned how to communicate across language and cultural barriers. You've learned how to manage or participate in multicultural project teams. You've found out how to work independently, take initiative, and, no doubt, use patience and flexibility in getting work done. Emphasize these accomplishments on your resume or CV.

Also use this time to update and polish your skills or to learn new ones. Register for on-line classes or local workshops. Attend conferences where you can network, make presentations, and find out about the latest industry trends.

Interview for Advertised Positions

Why wait until you're home to begin applying for work? Organizations can take weeks and even months to fill a vacancy. So if an advertised position catches your eye, be prepared to send in your application materials right away. Go back to Chapter 2 for suggestions on where to look for jobs. While that chapter dealt with the global job search, you'll find many of the same resources helpful when looking for work at home. Follow up on any leads that come your way. And prepare yourself for making and receiving telephone calls at odd hours, even in the middle of the night, because of international time differences.

Negotiate Your Contract

Once you've been offered a position you want to accept, the negotiating game begins again. The move back to your home country, if that's your next destination, should have been part of your original contract. If you're planning to globe hop to another international assignment, then you'll want to negotiate relocation expenses with your new international employer. Review Chapter 7 for suggestions on possible areas for negotiation.

A major advantage this time around will be the depth and breadth of experience you have gained during your current international assignment. Don't be shy. Capitalize on your sharpened global skills as you negotiate for your next assignment.

Consider Staying

Even though your international ticket is about to expire, that doesn't necessarily mean that you have to come back to your home country. Working globally can be addictive. You may decide to extend your expatriate status indefinitely or to see as much of the world as you can.

If your wanderlust is still in full throttle, explore the possibility of working for another firm in the same country overseas. The challenge comes in finding another company that will be willing and able to sponsor you. As Mike explains, "Often, you need a guaranteed job to obtain a commercial visa to even stay in a country. I found some resourceful individuals who had been in Hong Kong for a decade, simply moving from posting to posting. When I first went over there, I met quite a few of these people, but their numbers dwindled as Asia experienced its first serious [financial] downdraft in two decades." Although it might not be easy to find another position where you're based, if your heart is set on remaining abroad, you owe it to yourself to check out your options.

If you're not able to locate another position where you're already based overseas, consider alternative locations. Initiate another global job search from your international location. You might have additional considerations, such as having to move your family from one foreign place to another, but with adequate preparation and flexibility, you can rise to the challenge.

As you can see, the same strategies that worked for you in landing your dream job abroad can work for your return. Focus—Research—Network—Ask for Help—Prepare—Interview—Succeed! These steps will get you to your next domestic or global work assignment.

COMING HOME: SOFTENING THE CULTURAL BLOW

Even before you leave your international assignment, you can take a number of steps to successfully manage your transition home. Here are a few suggestions:

Involve Your Family

Just as you involved your family from the beginning in your plans to work abroad, it is important to involve them in the plans to return home. If you were wise, you negotiated for repatriation counseling in your original contract. If not, you still might be able to request assistance from your company.

With or without help from a counselor, start discussing and processing the feelings of family members *before* you go home. Some of the questions you might discuss together include:

- What have you enjoyed the most about our stay abroad?
- What was the most difficult adjustment you had to make?
- What have you missed most about home while living here?
- If you were to make the trip over again, what would you do differently?
- What will you miss the most about this place when we return home (or go on to our next adventure abroad)?
- What about home are you most looking forward to?
- How have you changed since living abroad?
- What did you learn during your time overseas—about yourself, other people, the host country, and the home country?
- What is your favorite food from the host country?
- How are you feeling about leaving here and returning home?
- Of all the things you did while you were here, what would you most like to do again?

- What has made you feel the happiest while living here?
- What have been the highlights of your stay abroad?
- What will you tell your friends at home about your overseas adventure?
- What do you imagine life will be like back at home (or in our next international location)?
- How have you benefited from our living abroad?

Add other questions that come to mind. By addressing the repatriation issue head-on, you'll remove many of your family members' fears and concerns.

Talk to Other Expatriates

Ask expatriates who have been in your situation what it was like to move home after working abroad. Arrange for them to talk to your family members. You can ask them the same questions you asked of your family and add the following:

- What was the hardest adjustment you had to make in moving home?
- What was the easiest adjustment you had to make?
- What would have made for a smoother transition?
- What do you wish you had done differently?
- What action did you take that helped your and your family's adjustment?
- What advice would you give to those who are about to return home?

The well of expatriate experience runs deep. People who have experience working abroad can be wonderful resources for you. Ask for their insights on how best to prepare yourself for coming home.

Stay Connected to Your Hosts

With the Internet and e-mail, it's easier than ever to stay in touch with those people you leave behind. Take advantage of technology to communicate with your new international friends and colleagues. Rather than simply drop out of sight and out of mind, keep plugged in to changes within the company and within the lives of your associates. The people you met while abroad are now part of your personal network—your now larger personal network.

Staying in touch with your international associates and your host country will help make your transition home easier. Corresponding via e-mail, for instance, will allow you to bring part of your overseas experience home with you. Cooking some of the foods or playing music from the host country will also ease your transition. Weave the strands of your adventure abroad into your new life back home.

Once home, try to schedule return visits to your host country. You might be able to swing these trips via company business. If not, make plans to go back on your own. Mike did just that. He had made a lot of friends during his two-year stay in Hong Kong, and he missed the excitement of living there. After he returned to the United States and settled in a new job, he went back to Hong Kong for a short visit. He felt renewed after catching up with his friends and taking in the sights and smells of his former city. Just knowing he could always return helped make his transition home more palatable.

In addition to returning to the host country if possible, invite friends you made abroad to visit *your* country. Many expatriates say that the friendships they made while living and working abroad are lasting ones. As Bill explains: "What struck me the most was that the friends I made overseas are friends for life. Maybe because you're all in the same situation, all foreigners in the same place, these are friends you can count on. When I had surgery in Jakarta, my friend flew in from Athens to be at my bedside. When my friend got sick, we flew into Hawaii to be with him."

Still another way for you to remain connected once you return home is to look for business opportunities between your host and home countries. For instance, you could consider starting an import business as Mark and Susan did. They spent two years in the Peace Corps in Thailand. When they returned home, they created a retail business, selling clothing and other products from Thailand. Similarly, John set up a small shop and gallery when he came home after several years in Japan. The business necessitates frequent trips to Japan, giving John and his wife a chance to visit the friends they made there.

Keep a Journal

Writers know that the process of writing helps clarify their thoughts and feelings. In her wonderful book, *The Artist's Way at Work*, author Julie

Cameron introduces readers to the concept of "morning pages." She encourages people to write three pages of notes in longhand first thing each morning. It doesn't matter what you write about, Cameron explains. But as you begin writing, trivial and mundane thoughts will give way to the powerful underlying hopes, fears, and concerns that drive your behavior.

The exercise offers a fabulous way to tap into your innermost thoughts and can be a helpful means for processing your feelings about returning home. Use your own morning pages or journal to record your impressions about coming back. Notice what strikes you most about your experience, and write about your observations.

Consider keeping a journal when you are traveling, living, and working abroad as well. Over time, it's easy to forget the highlights and challenges of your global adventures. By keeping a journal of your personal and professional recollections, you'll have a record that will help you recall and appreciate your experiences. By writing down sensory descriptions and bits and pieces about your daily life abroad, you will be able to revisit your stay overseas even after returning home. In this respect, you won't have to be totally removed from your international experience.

Seek Out the International Community

Expatriates speaking about returning home often mention the importance of choosing their new environment carefully. In making the move abroad, you might have moved from a small rural town in the United States to a large European city. You might have experienced severe culture shock in the process. But, having now made the adjustment to city life, you might not want to return to your small town back in the States.

The more international, energetic, and stimulating your home away from home was, the harder it may be for you to return to an isolated or homogenous community. Back in the United States, you might want to choose a home with a large international population. You might want to find a position that requires frequent international business travel.

For example, after living in Hong Kong, Mike chose not to return to the relatively quiet atmosphere of the Pacific Northwest. Instead he took a job in the thriving metropolis of Washington, D.C. Gail, too, moved to the D.C. area upon returning to the States because she wanted to continue working with U.S. government agencies. Marshall works in Singapore, but he is beginning to plan for his return to the United States. Because his wife is Japanese, he wants to live in a community where they both will feel welcome and have access to an Asian community. You should give serious consideration to your own needs and look for a community in which you can be comfortable and happy when you return home.

Seek Out Your Favorite Activities

When I worked in Cairo, two of the activities I missed most were hiking and browsing in bookstores. I also missed having space to myself. After I got home, I indulged myself by going on long hikes, alone or with a friend, for several consecutive weekends. I also combed bookstores for new treasures that had been published in my absence.

As you think about coming home, reflect on the activities that you've missed and have had to put on hold while you were away. Start making plans now to catch up on your favorite events, friendships, and activities. These plans will create excitement about coming home.

EXPATRIATES REFLECT ON THEIR EXPERIENCES

All the expatriates I interviewed said that if they had the chance to work globally again, they would. Despite the hassles, frustrations, and culture shock, all relished the opportunities they had had to see and work the world. When accompanied by family, they felt that their international work experience had been a positive way of bringing members closer together. All commented on what a life-changing event working globally had been, and several spoke of wanting to continue working overseas.

Jack has worked outside the United States almost his entire adult life, in such places as Vietnam, Libya, Australia, Qatar, Saudi Arabia, Egypt, and Japan. While he hasn't experienced the challenges of repatriation, he has witnessed others who have. He comments:

> It is fairly common for someone who seems to hate their overseas assignment and constantly talks of returning home to be reas-signed to the States. Once home, they find that their perception of the States has either changed or that life in the States suddenly seems different. These same people then realize that life overseas

was maybe better than they thought. Some even ask to return to the very same country they were complaining about. The fact is, working overseas changes people in some way, and most come to find they want no other way of life.

Gail came back from abroad with a greater appreciation of what she can do without in her life. She realized that she wants comfort and a little luxury. Yet she returned with a strong sense of what is enough for her, as opposed to wanting to have it all. This sentiment was echoed by Elena. For her, realizing what she could live without while abroad was both enlightening and liberating. She found she really didn't need all that much to be comfortable and at peace with herself.

Barry sums up his feelings about his overseas experience. He writes: "It can be quite an adventure. It can be lucrative. It can be the base for a lot of interesting and surprisingly inexpensive travel. Overseas work can be interesting, and it looks good on a resume. Expatriates are generally an outgoing, gregarious lot, and we have made many new friends."

Whatever your reasons for wanting to travel, live, and work abroad, take heart in the personal reflections of these expatriates. Prepare yourself for the adventure of a lifetime, a roller-coaster ride of emotions, and a richly rewarding turn of events.

WHAT WILL YOU DO NEXT?

Before continuing on to the next chapter, take these steps to reach your dream of living and working abroad:

- Focus your job search for your next assignment, either at home or abroad. Decide where you want to live and for whom you want to work.
- Assess the new knowledge, skills, and personal attributes that you've gained by working globally.
- Research the global job market for available positions and hiring trends.
- Contact company insiders, search consultants, and mentors for advice on reentering the domestic job market or continuing to work overseas.

- Create a success support group with other returning expatriates.
- Update your international resume.
- Draft a new cover letter that you can then tailor for specific positions.
- Take classes to update your skills for your next work assignment.
- Use the questions presented in this chapter as a springboard for a family discussion about repatriation.
- Talk with other expatriates about their repatriation experiences.
- Gather addresses of friends with whom you want to stay in touch once you return home.
- Keep a journal during your stay abroad and upon returning home.

10

Get Insider Information—Learn!

Learn from the mistakes made by others because you will not live long enough to make them all yourself.
—Marshall, Executive Director, Asia-Pacific

"**D**o I need to know a second language to work abroad?" "I'm over 45 years old—will I have a problem finding work abroad?" "What can I expect in working with an international search firm?" "How can I help my spouse locate a job when I'm sent on an international assignment?" These are among some of the most frequently asked questions from people seeking international employment. In this chapter, you'll receive answers to these questions and others. You will also receive advice on staying motivated during your international job search, suggestions from expatriates who've already succeeded, and tips for success—from A to Z.

FREQUENTLY ASKED QUESTIONS

Foreign Languages
Do I need to speak a second language to work overseas?
No. There are thousands of short- and long-term jobs abroad for people who speak English only. Once you zero in on your dream work overseas, you can investigate whether or not you'll need a second language to get

where you want to go. If you're in international sales, in all likelihood, you'll need to speak the language of your customers. If you're planning to teach English, most likely you won't. As Marshall, an expatriate who lived in Asia for several years, explains: "It's more important to understand the culture than to be fluent in the language."

However, if you ask me if you *should* learn a second language, regardless of job requirements, my answer is, *Mais oui*! Yes! There's no better way to begin your awareness and understanding of another culture, its values, and its customs. By caring enough to learn another language, you'll demonstrate respect for people of cultures different from your own. You'll also learn alternatives for problem solving and team building. Even if you learn only a few simple words and phrases, your experiences overseas will be so much richer than those of someone who doesn't. You'll be able to understand more of the culture, open doors, and develop stronger relationships with the people around you.

What's the best foreign language for me to learn? That depends on where you're going and what work you'll be doing. Another way to answer this question is to determine which language speaks *to you*. If you enjoy a language, you'll be motivated to master it, despite the obstacles and difficulties.

Why study Chinese if you have no interest in the Chinese culture or people? It's a mistake to study a language merely because it might be useful in job opportunities later on. First, there's no guarantee you'll enjoy the language. Second, today's "hot" languages are often passé tomorrow. Imagine spending lots of sweat and energy mastering a language that you're not crazy about. Then, by the time you're able to use it proficiently, you discover that it's no longer in demand. But if you like the language *and* see promising opportunities to use it ahead, go for it!

What languages are "hot" now? English and Spanish continue to be the most popular languages for study in North America. At the Berlitz School of Languages in New York City, English tops the list. In the Pacific Northwest, Spanish is followed in popularity by French, Italian, and Japanese. The Modern Language Association reports that the greatest and most consistent growth in study is in Chinese and Japanese.

Interesting, *n'est-ce pas*? While it's fascinating to learn which languages are currently in demand, remember your own objectives in seeking work abroad and study the language that will best help you reach them.

What's the best way to learn a second language? Let's start

with your motivation. Why do you want to study a particular language? How will you use it? For work? For traveling? For both? Begin your course of study with a strong desire and a clear objective. Once you're in touch with your passion for learning another language, don't just dip your toe in the water. Immerse yourself in the language totally. Take the plunge and go for a swim! Learn by doing. Live the language. Breathe it. If you haven't seen the film *Breaking Away*, rent it today. Use your new language 24 hours a day, even when you're sleeping. Practice. Practice. Practice.

If you can study the language in the country where it's spoken, so much the better. If not, sign up for classes in your area and practice using the language at every available opportunity. Supplement your classes with language tapes and foreign films. Join a language or culture club through which you can meet people who speak the language you're learning.

If you end up studying the language in a country in which it's spoken, start by learning basic greetings and phrases that will help you meet people: *hello, goodbye, please, thank you, yes, no, pardon me, don't worry about it, how are you?, I'm fine, cheers.* Learn the do's and don'ts of the gestures that accompany the language. Then learn words and phrases that will help you order meals in a restaurant, travel around the area, use banking and mailing services, and do your shopping. Once you make an attempt to speak even a little of the local language, you'll be amazed at the warm welcome you'll receive. Soon you'll feel right at home.

What language programs do you recommend? Consider applying

for an accelerated language program that provides a total immersion and experiential format. Before choosing any program, however, ask a few questions: How many students will be in your class? What's the teacher/ student ratio? Obviously, individual or small classes will be more expensive than larger classes. An optimum size for learning and participation is generally 9 to 12 students.

How long are the class sessions? Can you join the program at any time or are there definite start and end dates? Naturally, you'll have more flexibility in your schedule if you can enroll in classes at your convenience. However, you might have a difficult time adjusting to the level of a class in progress. A school with a set schedule forces you to make a definite commitment for the duration of the program.

Ask about the student population. What is the ratio of male to female students? What is the age range of the participants? What countries are they from? You might prefer a language program with participants who are close to you in age, or a mix of men and women as opposed to only one gender.

What is the instructor's background? Of course, you'll want to know that the teacher is qualified to present the program. Your first thought might be to prefer a native speaker. That way, you figure, you'll get the flavor of the language that only a native speaker can bring. But just because a teacher has native fluency in a language doesn't guarantee that he or she can *teach* it. You'll want a teacher with enthusiasm, but teaching skills do not start and end there. How much experience does the instructor have? What are his or her credentials?

What methodology does the instructor use? You might be familiar with the saying, "What I hear, I forget. What I see, I remember. What I do, I understand." The saying applies strongly to the study of language. Look for an interactive, experiential, and highly participatory program. If your primary goal is to communicate with native speakers, you'll need to at least speak and understand the language. If you have the time and opportunity to add grammar (groan), reading, and writing to your studies, do so. You'll be that much further ahead in opening the lines of communication.

If you're considering a residential-style program, ask about housing options. Will you live in a dormitory, a private home with a local family, or an apartment? How close are the accommodations to the school itself? What other amenities and cultural opportunities are available?

What is the overall cost of the program? Do a cost analysis of all the programs you're considering. Don't forget to include the cost of supplementary materials, room and board, travel, and incidentals.

Working Papers

What kind of documents do I need to work in another country and how do I get them? Typically, you'll need a passport, business visa, and work permit to work in another country. Because requirements change periodically, it's a good idea to check with embassies and consulates for the most current regulations.

If you're 18 or older and a full-time student, you can apply for a special work permit through the Council on International Education Exchange (CIEE). This permit allows you to pursue short-term work (generally from 3 to 12 months, depending on the country) and is not renewable. Currently, the CIEE provides work permits for Australia, Canada, Costa Rica, France, Germany, Ireland, and New Zealand. See Chapter 7 for more information on the type of paperwork you will need for employment outside the United States.

I'm already living in the country where I want to work. Can I apply for advertised jobs and then get my work permit? You could very well enter a country on a tourist visa and receive a job offer once you're there. However, you'll still need to return to the United States to complete the paperwork required for your work permit.

How long will it take to get my work permit? If your international employer is filing the paperwork for your work documents, or if you're applying for short-term employment through the CIEE, it generally takes about a month to six weeks to receive your work permit. If you're completing the paperwork yourself, it may take considerably longer to receive the documents, simply because you'll be unfamiliar with the application process.

Is it possible to get work abroad without a work permit? Anything is possible. Expatriates sometimes work "under the table" or "on the gray market"—mostly in temporary jobs. Is it worth being deported or paying hefty fines if you're caught? Personally, I don't think so. The fact that "everybody does it" is no guarantee you won't be caught and forced to pay the penalty for working illegally.

Diversity Issues

I'm over 45 years old. Will I have a problem finding work abroad? Yes and no. For some jobs, some countries, and some industries, age will be a limiting factor. But many employers will welcome your experience and maturity. For example, the most prestigious positions with the United Nations require considerable experience. Senior-level UN positions often go to those advanced in age. So direct your search toward positions in which age is an advantage. University professorships and executive-level management jobs are two examples.

Realistically, when is someone too old to find work overseas? You're not too old to find work overseas until you're too old to travel! The truth is, some international employers and recruiters will make assumptions, on the basis of age, about an applicant's ability to perform a particular job. Don't let this prejudice stop you from seeking your dream work abroad. By following the steps in this book, you'll be poised to get around this and other obstacles.

I saw an ad for a position with the Central Intelligence Agency that said applicants must be younger than age 35. I thought age discrimination was illegal in the United States. How can the CIA get away with this? It's difficult to answer your question without knowing more about the specific position. It's possible that the age limit was a bona fide requirement for the job. Perhaps it was an undercover position requiring the employee to match a profile that included a specific age range. Otherwise, it is not legal for U.S. government agencies to discriminate against candidates because of age.

I'm disabled. Will this prevent me from being considered for an overseas assignment? It could, or it may make no difference to the person hiring you. Just as people of differing abilities have to fight for access to jobs in the United States, people often have to fight for employment access abroad. Here are a few steps you can take to overcome this potential barrier: Keep building your network of contacts, seek out personal referrals for international assignments, and reiterate your willingness and ability to travel overseas at every appropriate opportunity. It takes tremendous energy, but your efforts can help dispel many preconceived ideas that others may have about your inability to work abroad successfully.

Recruiters
What can I expect when working with an international search firm? Since the search firm, or "headhunter," basically works for the employer, you can expect to pay no fees for its services. Rather, the employer pays the search firm when a suitable employee is found. (An employment agency, which generally places people in entry-level positions, does charge job hunters a fee for its services, however). In many cases, the headhunter or search firm will counsel you on your resume and the interview process and will keep you posted on the status of your job applications.

Family Matters
Will international employers view my family as a benefit or a detriment? Once again, the answer depends on several factors. For employers, it's costly to relocate an entire family overseas. At the same time, your family can be viewed as a source of stability and contentment for you while you're posted overseas, especially if they are experienced international travelers and eager to move abroad with you. If your family members are unable to adapt to the international environment successfully, however, they can jeopardize the longevity of your assignment. Sending you or family members home early will cost the company even more money.

How can I help prepare my family for moving overseas?
Involve your family from the beginning in your quest to find work globally. Include each family member in discussions and solicit each one's feedback, questions, and concerns. If you do land an assignment, negotiate for predeparture cross-cultural training for your family and participate in the sessions. When your plans are presented as a family adventure with benefits for everyone, members are more likely to buy in and get excited about the trip.

How can I help my spouse locate a job when I'm sent on an international assignment? Ask your hiring organization for assistance.

For starters, maybe the company can employ your spouse on a part- or full-time basis, or as a consultant. Of course, the company might not have any open positions for which your partner is qualified. In this case, perhaps the company could contact other organizations in the area that might have positions available. If neither of these options is feasible, negotiate with the employer for career-transition counseling for your partner.

General Questions

Will I have difficulty reentering the U.S. job market after a stint abroad? You might, so it's good to prepare yourself for that possibility. See the previous chapter for more detailed information on how to position yourself for the domestic job market after working abroad.

Everyone talks about the value of networking, but I'm not very good at it. What can I do to improve my comfort level and ability to network? You're not alone. Many of us suffer anxieties about networking, sometimes called the old "meet and greet." But networking is a skill that can be learned and enhanced, just like riding a bicycle or playing golf.

The best way to overcome your anxieties about networking is to prepare ahead of time and to practice your skills as often as possible. Set specific goals for professional events—to introduce yourself to three people you've never met before, for example. Prepare a few questions to ask others. You'll find that if you concentrate on others and ask about what's important to them—rather than thinking about your own nervousness—a lot of your anxiety will melt away. By all means, though, be prepared to tell the people you meet about your specific goals for working globally.

Networking is like shopping: It's a lot easier to maintain your wardrobe if you make regular purchases over time than if you try to fill your closet all at once. If you build your wardrobe gradually, you'll be prepared when a special event comes along—you'll already have the right outfit. You won't end up standing in front of your closet on the eve of the event bemoaning: "I've got nothing to wear." Networking is just the same. Don't wait until you need help finding work abroad to build your personal and professional relationships. (For more information on networking for global employment, see Chapter 3.)

Are there any drawbacks to traveling, living, and working overseas? Oliver Wendell Holmes claimed: "A mind once stretched can never return to its original dimension." Indeed, after working abroad, you won't be the same person you were before. Traveling, living, and working abroad will broaden your horizons in ways you cannot even imagine. You'll experience exponential personal and professional growth. You'll see the world while sharpening your business skills. You'll make money that will help finance your travels. You'll discover firsthand the similarities and differences among people from other cultures.

Drawbacks? Sure. You run the risk of having your core assumptions and beliefs challenged almost on a daily basis. You risk ending relationships with those who feel threatened by or are uncomfortable with the ways you've changed when you go home. You may risk the loss of influence in your company because of your distance from headquarters. You may have difficulty even reentering the domestic job market after a stint overseas. Your children who accompany you overseas may miss seeing their grandparents. These potential risks and losses, however, are greatly outweighed by the benefits of living and working globally.

In which countries and industries is it easiest to find international employment? Currently, promising work opportunities are available in Eastern Europe, Latin America, and Africa. Respondents to the 1999 NFTC survey identified Brazil, China, and Mexico as the top three emerging locations for international assignments. Opportunities and locations are subject to change, of course, depending on social, political, and economic upheavals.

Teaching English, international trade, construction and engineering, small business development, travel and tourism, health care, and environmental services are growing global industries. (For more information on emerging markets and industries, see Chapter 2.)

I'd love to work on a cruise ship. Where do I start? One of my earliest dreams was to join the Good Samaritan ship *Hope* as a nurse and then travel to exotic ports of call. By the time I was old enough to choose a career, however, I opted for teaching rather than nursing, and the *Hope* was no longer in service.

Fortunately for you, there are still a number of opportunities to work aboard cruise lines. Assignments are generally short-term (from 4 to 12 months) and involve a variety of positions—everything from aerobics instructor to entertainer to ship's physician. Start your search by deciding where you want to travel and what kind of job you want. Then scope out the various cruise lines.

Do I need to be certified to teach English overseas? No, you don't. However, you're likely to have more job opportunities and better pay if you are certified to teach English. A number of certification programs are available—both in the United States and overseas.

How do I go about starting my own import/export business? Starting your own import/export business can be fun and profitable if you research your product market carefully before investing. First, decide where you'd like to travel and do business. Next, find out what products are readily available in the host country and would sell well at home. Consider what merchandise you have access to at home that would sell well in the countries where you want to do business.

Once you decide on your product line, check with the U.S. Department of Commerce or your state international trade agency. Find out what licensing you'll need to start your business. Then you're on your way!

What are my chances of really being able to work abroad? By following the easy steps outlined in this book, maintaining your motivation, and developing an action plan, you *can* find work in the global marketplace.

BREAKING THROUGH THE BARRIERS

Remember that finding international employment can take from 6 to 12 months. During that time, it's easy to lose heart. You can't be certain that your efforts will result in a job offer. How can you stay motivated during this time so that you *can* reach your goal? Let's review a few of the success strategies we've learned so far and then add a few more.

Stay Focused on Your Goal

Remember what work you want to do globally and, most importantly, re-member *why* you want to do it. You'll be able to maintain perspective and balance during the ups and downs of your global job search if you "keep your eyes on the prize." Continue to believe in your skills and abilities no matter what obstacles you face. If you haven't made a Treasure Map, make one now. (See Chapter 1 for details.) Put your Treasure Map in a place where you can see it every day. Let it be a visual reminder of your global job quest.

Ask for Help When You Need It

You don't have to undertake your international job search alone—and you shouldn't. You would miss out on the benefits of other people's experience. Ask your mentor, research librarians, and others in your personal network for their advice when you get stuck. Ask sooner rather than later to help maximize your research and planning time. Set yourself up for success by attending your support group meetings regularly. Ask other members for feedback and suggestions.

Do the Work

You can do all the research, ask and receive advice, and build an extended support network. But unless you're willing to do the follow-up and follow-through, all your hard work will end there. Only by applying yourself wholeheartedly to your goal can you achieve the success you imagine.

Make a daily commitment to yourself to do the work. Set daily, weekly, and monthly goals for your global job search, then monitor your progress toward success. Act on the advice you receive, follow up on leads, and prepare your global work portfolio. Be willing to do what it takes to reach your dream of working in faraway places. Through consistency, dis-cipline, and persistence you can make it overseas.

Review Your Success Portfolio

In Chapter 5, you learned how to create a "success portfolio," which we described as an extensive promotional packet. One of the benefits of this portfolio is that it can serve as a visual reminder of your professional accomplishments.

It's easy to become discouraged when international jobs don't come your way. I'm willing to bet, however, that at some other time in your career, you faced similar disappointments but then succeeded down the road. Spend some time looking through your success portfolio. Reflect on your accomplishments and the obstacles you had to overcome to succeed. Then, remember, if you succeeded once, you can do it again—this time to reach your goal of working globally.

Use Positive Self-Talk

Unfortunately, many of us have perfected the art of putting ourselves down. We kick ourselves over things we wished we had or hadn't said, missed opportunities, mistakes we've made, or how long it took us to learn a new skill. Not only do we beat ourselves up for things that happened in the past but we also set ourselves up for defeat before we even get started. We tell ourselves: I can't do that. I'm too shy. I'm too young. I'm too old.

But the way you talk to yourself can be a powerful motivator, or demotivator, depending on what you tell yourself and how you say it. Your messages to yourself can also make a difference in the results you get. For example, Karen had been under considerable stress at work. She'd been putting in a lot of overtime and dealing with a difficult coworker. A few weeks later, I met her for breakfast and commented on how happy and relaxed she looked, considering what she'd been going through. When I asked what had changed, she responded that she had had a "heart-to-heart talk with herself." Realistically, she knew that her workload and coworker's behavior were not going to change anytime soon. To cope, she realized that she was going to have to change her attitude. Specifically, she told herself the benefits of her working overtime, and she began to focus on what she *liked* about her coworker. To her surprise and relief, the strategy actually began to work. She started to feel better about going to work, and it showed.

The words we tell ourselves *do* make a difference. To work effectively, think of these three Rs: *Refine* the words you use, *root* them in reality, and *repeat* them often. In refining your words, choose positive language and use the present tense as if your words were fact. For example, you might say, "I am mastering my ability to understand spoken French more each day," rather than "What's the matter with me? I'll never be able to speak French." Your positive words should not be unreasonable, however. "I'm speaking fluent French in just six weeks" is clearly unrealistic.

Some experts say that an adult learner must hear something about 19 times before the message is remembered and becomes part of the subconscious. Once you've chosen positive and realistic phrases, therefore, repeat them often. Post them on your refrigerator or bathroom mirror. Make tapes of these messages and listen to them while you go for a walk or drive your car. The stated beliefs will soon become part of your subconscious.

Listen to Motivational Tapes and Music

In addition to the tapes of positive self-talk that you make for yourself, investigate motivational tape series produced by successful sales and service professionals. Any number of tapes on the market can help you stay focused, energized, and optimistic while you seek work abroad. Look for coaches who can share the secrets of what's worked for them, regardless of their goals. Use their proven models to produce equally effective results.

You might also feel inspired and motivated by music. My favorites include the theme music from *The Right Stuff* and *The Hunt for Red October* for determination and John Williams's *Fanfare for the Los Angeles Olympics* for inspiration. For music to work by, my favorites include Bach's cello suites, Heinrich Biber's *Rosary Sonatas* (16 violin sonatas from the early Baroque era), solo piano music by George Winston and Michael Jones, and Latin American or Spanish guitar music. My choices depend on my moods, as I'm sure yours do. Find out what type of music relaxes, inspires, and motivates you.

Read Inspirational Biographies

In the summer of 1999, Lance Armstrong of the U.S. Postal Service Team won the Tour de France, the world's most grueling bicycle race. Armstrong's story is especially poignant not only because he won the famous race but also because he overcame incredible odds to do so. In 1996 he was diagnosed with testicular cancer that had already spread to his liver and brain. Yet, he battled his way back, overcoming self-doubt and the doubts of his fellow cyclists in the process, to win the coveted award.

After reading stories like Lance Armstrong's, I'm inspired to overcome any obstacles preventing me from achieving success. What about you? Read biographies of people who have made remarkable comebacks and demonstrated tremendous grace under fire or whose courageous spirit inspired others to follow their paths. Learn from their life lessons to stay motivated when you're ready to give up your dream of landing a job overseas.

Create a Positive Work Environment

Find a place you can call your own to set up your global job-search operations. Then fill the space with all the elements you need to be your most productive self. Ask yourself what would make your space comfortable and convenient. For many of us, ample and varied lighting, proximity to resources, and ergonomically designed office furniture and workstations are important. Your choice of room colors also has tremendous impact on your creativity and energy, so choose carefully. You're the only one who knows what the best work environment is for you.

Try to create a supportive and motivating environment in which you can work effectively, free of distractions, interruptions, and worries. It's nice if you can create the ideal work environment, but I know it's not always possible. Setting up such an office may not be economically feasible, or you may even lack a room to call your own. Don't let this obstacle deter you from accomplishing your goal. You can improvise for the time being—set up a mobile office at your dining room table or the local public library. Author Ann Rule described her work environment early in her career. She'd write at the kitchen table, with her small children running underfoot. Somehow she managed to get published regardless. Despite the obstacles you face in your work setting, you can reach your goals, too.

Stay Healthy

It's difficult to perform at your best when your health is an issue of concern. Think of what you can do each day to fuel your body, mind, and spirit. You'll increase your personal effectiveness significantly if you take care of yourself the way you should: get enough sleep; eat a healthy, balanced diet; get plenty of fresh air and exercise. When you take time for play breaks and rejuvenate your senses, it's easier to come back to previous problems with a different perspective.

If you can, create a time and space when you do nothing but pamper yourself—that's frosting on the cake. By allowing a way for creative ideas to bubble to the surface, you may gain new insights in approaching your global job search.

TIPS FROM EXPATRIATES

In my interviews with overseas adventurers, I asked what advice they would give to others who wanted to work globally. Here's what they said:

For Employees Accepting International Assignments

"Always strive to build relationships with locals. These relationships will change your life significantly. I have watched many expats stick with their friends and family from their own country and truly miss the life experiences in their host country! Find someone your age, in your field, in your industry, and interview that person.... People love to tell you about themselves, and generally people enjoy helping others. Investigate the differences in businesses based on your questions and discussions with this person. Then ask the person to recommend someone else you should speak with—maybe someone older and at a higher level in the organization. The Internet is a good tool for discovering the resources available to you in these areas. But always let it lead you to someone to speak to!" *(Debra, Management Consultant, Europe)*

"Make sure it's a job you love. Really examine your motives for going abroad because even though it's exciting, you're also going to be spending time there. Learn the language. Learn how little you can live with. It's liberating to let go of a lot of your material things. It was definitely enriching for my marriage because we shared the entire process together. Think about what you're going to do when you get back. Be very honest about your flexibility. Are you flexible by nature or not?" *(Elena, Consultant, Paris)*

"Be flexible and always remind yourself that this is an adventure. No matter what happens, it will make a great story someday. Enjoy the challenges that present themselves. Have an open mind and get out and explore. Be adventurous with eating and take advantage of whatever food is the specialty in that country. Language helps. You need a commitment to do what it takes to get there and be willing to do without." *(Gail, U.S. Civil Service, Germany)*

"Make sure you know what you're getting yourself into. Make sure you go over first and that your spouse goes with you. Go in with open eyes. Make sure you understand what your job is and what your job responsibilities are. Don't go in like I did and think, if it works in New York City, it'll work anywhere in the world. . . . You still have to have the locals. Ask for suggestions. Have regular staff meetings. Give feedback. Think global. Act local." *(Bill, Vice President of International Human Resources)*

"Have the desire to be in the country because your attitude will be apparent. In someone else's country, know and respect the laws. For example, in the United States it's safe to speak out against the government, but in Singapore, it's not. Be interested in learning and be willing to take a back seat until you understand the culture. Associate with the local population." *(Marshall, International Sales Manager, Asia)*

"To succeed in Japan, you need tolerance, patience, and deep pockets. The first year of doing business, you're still in shock, busy fighting the system and trying to survive. In the second year, you start to get in the groove. You ask more intelligent and relevant questions, and you may have a connection or two. It takes a year to build a relationship. In the third and fourth years, you begin to absorb more of the language and culture." *(Marshall, International Sales Manager, Asia)*

"Go over on an unplanned trip first. Visit local markets and eat out. If you want to know the people, see what they eat. Educate yourself about the country and culture before you go." *(Cheri, Director of International Human Resources)*

"Go with a credible agency and one that will support you, especially in China. It helps to know you have an agency that understands and supports you." *(Bonnie, English Teacher, China)*

For Family Members Accompanying Employees on International Assignments

"It's a good idea for the partner to think a little about what she or he wants to do while living abroad. If you want to work, exploring opportunities and making contacts in the United States ahead of time might prove useful. I found it beneficial to read about the country and culture to which I was moving. This reading included guidebooks, books written for expats, and books that focused on the political, economic, social, and cultural aspects. If possible, talk with other expats who have lived in that country.... Make the most of the time you have, and don't put off doing things you really want to see or experience." *(Harriet, Asia)*

"You can go to a foreign country, but you don't have to be lonely. There are always so many organizations you can get involved in. Be sure and bring your own medications since you might not be able to find the same ones overseas. Our family bonded much more and became closer during our time overseas because we only had each other in the beginning to rely on." *(Kris, Paris)*

"Many professional organizations can help with your transition, whatever your field may be. There are professional societies—Independent Professionals Network, Human Resources Society, Petro Chemical Engineers Society.... Many cities also have special organizations focused directly on individuals in this situation. For example, FOCUS has chapters in most major European cities. The American Chamber of Commerce has chapters across Europe. Use the Internet to locate these organizations, then find a person to call and begin your networking process. Attend all of their meetings; subscribe to their newsletters." *(Debra, Management Consultant, Europe)*

For Those Going into Business for Themselves

"Knowledge of the language is essential if you are in business for yourself. Use local legal help to obtain permits. They usually will know how to get things done. Do not rely on yourself. It is not the United States, and things are not usually done in the same organized way. Study the market." *(Craig, Business Consultant, Spain)*

"Be interested in the local people. It's an instant turn-off if you go with the attitude that you are going to enlighten them. From cab drivers to hotel personnel, ask questions to get to know them better.... I wish I'd known more about cultural differences, such as the Australian view of time, before I went. If I were going back again, I'd be better prepared and know more about the local people than I did." *(Winston, Professional Speaker, Australia)*

For International Recruiters, Managers, and Executives

"Network with others who are doing business in the host country.
Set up appointments through U.S.-based attorneys with offices in the host
country. Meet with employees' family members to answer questions
and address expectations and concerns about the overseas assignment.
When you interview applicants from other countries, ask more people to
validate what you hear and ask more kinds of questions. This will help
you overcome difficulties caused by cross-cultural differences." *(Cherie,
Director of International Human Resources)*

A TO Z TIPS FOR FINDING AN INTERNATIONAL ASSIGNMENT

ASK for help when you need it. You have tremendous resources available
to you, and people are generally more than happy to help you get what you
want. Prepare questions ahead of time for informational interviews. Keep
your questions, and the length of your appointment, to a minimum so as
not to impose on the person you're interviewing.

ATTEND professional meetings and conferences to connect with others
in your field. They may be able to refer you to important contacts and international assignments. Check with professional associations for their
schedules of conferences and conventions. For even greater visibility, sub-
mit a proposal for presentation at a conference.

BE CAREFUL when using so-called employment agencies. Many agencies charge a fee, without a guarantee of finding you work overseas. Instead, your fee buys you only a list of nonprofit organizations, companies,
or educational institutions. You could have discovered many of these organizations on your own.

CONTACT anyone who may be able to assist in your global job search.
Update your personal network database regularly, deleting and adding
names as appropriate.

DON'T expect to find an international position overnight (although anything is possible). Do expect to devote considerable time and research to finding your ideal international position. Remember, your goal is to find the right global assignment for you.

ESTABLISH an informal network with others seeking international employment. Get in touch regularly—either one-on-one or as a support group—to share information and suggestions. When your overseas assignment nears completion, develop another support network of expatriates who are also planning to return home soon. You can help each other through the process by sharing your feelings and plans for the transition.

ENVISION your ideal international position, then start preparing to make your vision a reality. Use the suggested visualizing techniques to make your dream of working internationally come true.

FOCUS your job search on what you want to do, where you want to do it, and for whom you want to work. There's nothing wrong with not knowing exactly what you want initially. But the sooner you can narrow your goal the better. Focusing will save you time in every phase of your global job search. You'll know what to research, the type of questions to ask and to whom, and what to do with the information you gather.

GO on informational interviews to obtain a better understanding of the type of job you want and the kind of organization for which you want to work. To gain a greater perspective on what it's like to live and work overseas, go on at least three informational interviews.

HAVE clear, realistic expectations of the position and living conditions you'll encounter before committing yourself to any overseas job offers. Ask specific and pointed questions of your prospective international employer to make sure that you know what you're getting yourself into.

INQUIRE about the job specifics, such as responsibilities, length of contract, salary and benefits, working papers, home-office support, and so forth, before accepting an offer abroad.

JOB HUNT in the United States to locate your ideal international position. It's possible to find international work once you get abroad, but you'll need to leave the country to get your work permit. Job hunt from abroad when you're ready to move on to your next international assignment or to come home.

KNOW your strengths and weaknesses when considering a particular job. Knowing your strengths gives you confidence. Knowing where you need to improve provides the impetus for personal and professional training and development.

LIMIT your global job search to a specific geographical region, type of organization, or type of work. Limiting your search will help decrease the amount of time, money, and effort it takes to locate an international job.

MARKET your personal attributes, such as your ability to cope in foreign cultures as well as your job-specific skills and experience, to potential employers. International employers want to know that you can adapt and succeed in a foreign culture. Show them you can.

NEVER work abroad without securing the necessary authorization papers such as a business visa and work permit. Working globally without the proper documentation puts you at risk for deportation and hefty fines.

ORGANIZE your international job search and make a daily, weekly, and monthly schedule of goals. An organized plan will help you move more quickly toward your goal of getting a job overseas. With a schedule, you can monitor your progress regularly and make alterations in your search as needed.

PREPARE for the move ahead by studying the language and culture of the host country. The more you know about where you're going, the faster you'll be able to adapt and get up to speed in performance. You'll also build relationships with the local population more quickly when you show a genuine interest in your new environment.

QUESTION your motivation for wanting an international job before beginning your job search. Be certain that your desire is strong enough to sustain you for the length of your search and the duration of your stay overseas.

READ trade journals, local and national newspapers, and magazines to find international job leads and to stay current with hiring and business trends. Read as much as possible about the local culture and people to minimize your culture shock once you're abroad.

SEND thank-you letters to those who have helped in your international job search and return the favor whenever possible. The gesture shows that you are gracious, appreciative, and thoughtful—all personal traits that will linger in the mind of the recipient.

TRADE information that you have uncovered in your global job search with those in your informal international network. Help each other to avoid reinventing the wheel. You can even be more systematic about sharing information—divvy up your research, then get back together and share your discoveries.

USE all available resources and contacts that can help you find work overseas. Don't ignore any possible leads in your quest for international employment.

VOICE your concerns if you have reservations about accepting a particular job offer. Don't wait until you've accepted an assignment and relocated abroad. By then, it's most likely too late to make any changes to your contract. Take care of yourself and your needs up front.

WRITE for information that can help you in your job search, but don't send out a lot of cover letters and resumes that haven't been requested. Target your inquiries based on what you uncover in your research. Write in your journal daily to help clarify your vision and motivation for working abroad. Use your journal to map your progress toward your goal. Finally, keep a journal to capture your feelings about working internationally and returning home.

XEROX and pass on information that may be useful to members of your informal professional network. Make sure you follow copyright laws when you do.

YIELD any unrealistic expectations you may have about living and working overseas. Why set yourself up for major disappointment and heartbreak?

ZERO in on your global work goals and set deadlines for achieving the steps that will lead you to the job you want.

WHAT WILL YOU DO NEXT?

The call of traveling, living, and working abroad speaks to adventurers and discoverers alike. You've obviously heard that call in one fashion or another or you wouldn't have picked up this book. Now you have everything you need to answer that call.

Of course, there will always be people who want to tell you that something is wrong with your dream of working globally. They'll tell you that the trend is to hire local nationals instead of expatriates, that compensation packages aren't as sweet today as they were 20 years ago, and that you'll have a hard time reentering the workforce at home at the end of your stay. They're right in the sense that trends in working globally do change and that coming home can be difficult. But never let naysayers discourage you from reaching your dream of working internationally.

Through this book, you've gained insights and inspiration from the personal journeys of those who have gone abroad before you. You've received practical information on how you can follow in their footsteps. The rest is up to you. Remember, the person who succeeds in working abroad is the one who is willing to invest the resources into seeing his or her vision through to actualization. You must be willing to exert the effort, create the connections, and take the time to make your own way around the world. Once you're ready, grab your bags, open your heart, and head for faraway places. Adventures and treasures abound. Bon voyage!

Appendix A
Recommended Reading

In selecting these resources, I purposely chose publications issued since 1995, with a few exceptions. My intent is to help you start your research with the most current information available.

PROFESSIONAL AND PERSONAL DEVELOPMENT

Creative Visualization—by Shakti Gawain (New World Library, 1995)

How to Work a Room: Learn the Strategies of Savvy Socializing For Business and Personal Success—by Susan Roane (Warner Books, 1989)

I Could Do Anything If I Only Knew What It Was—by Barbara Sher (Delacorte Press, 1995). Designed for readers who are searching for purpose in work and life

It's Only Too Late If You Don't Start Now: How to Create Your Second Life After Forty—by Barbara Sher (Delacorte Press, 1998). Gives guidance to readers who want to make significant life changes after age 40

Live the Life You Love: In Ten Easy Step-by-Step Lessons—by Barbara Sher (Bantam Doubleday Dell, 1997). Provides specific steps to help you uncover and realize your dreams

The Secrets of Savvy Networking: How to Make the Best Connections for Business and Personal Success—by Susan Roane (Warner Books, 1993)

The 7 Habits of Highly Effective People—by Stephen Covey (Simon & Schuster, 1989)

Teamworks! Building Support Groups That Guarantee Success—by Barbara Sher (Warner Books, 1989)

Think and Grow Rich—by Napoleon Hill (Ballantine Books, 1996)

What Color Is Your Parachute? A Practical Manual for Job-Hunters and Career-Changers—by Richard Nelson Bolles (Ten Speed Press, 2000). The best-known general career resource manual on the market, filled with exercises to help you plan your next career move. Uses a spiritual frame of reference in presenting information.

Work with Passion, How to Do What You Love for a Living—by Nancy Anderson (New World Library, 1995). Lots of valuable exercises, tips, and personal stories to help you discover your life's work

INTERNATIONAL EMPLOYMENT

Alternative Travel Directory: The Complete Guide to Work, Study and Travel Overseas—David Cline and Clayton A. Hubbs, editors (Transitions Abroad Publishing, 1999)

The Back Door Guide to Short Term Job Adventures: Internships, Extraordinary Experiences, Seasonal Jobs, Volunteering, Work Abroad—by Michael Landes (Ten Speed Press, 1997). A directory of resources, including names and addresses, for short-term, unconventional job opportunities, with some tips on getting started

The Canadian Guide to Working and Living Overseas—by Jean-Marc Hachey (University of Toronto Press, 1998)

Chez Vous En France; Living and Working in France—by Genevieve Brame (Kogan Page, 1999)

The Directory of Jobs and Careers Abroad—Jonathan Packer, editor (Vacation Work, 1997)

Great Jobs Abroad—by Arthur H. Bell (McGraw-Hill Book Company, 1997). A directory of business, government, and organizational contacts for those seeking work abroad. The book also gives general advice on finding work overseas.

The Grown-Up's Guide to Running Away from Home—by Rosanne Knorr (Ten Speed Press, 1998). Guidance for adults who want to start over in another part of the world. Gives practical information on closing up shop, transporting belongings and family, and finding a new home overseas.

How to Get a Job in Europe—by Robert Sanborn and Cherly Matherly (Surrey Books, 1999). Includes a country-by-country look at what and where the jobs are in Europe

International Job Finder: Where the Jobs Are Worldwide—by Sue Cubbage and Marcia Williams (Planning Communications, 1998)

International Jobs Directory—by Ronald Krannich and Carly Rae (Impact Publications, 1999)

International Jobs—Where They Are, How to Get Them—by Eric Kocher (Perseus Books, 1999). Primarily a directory of businesses and non-profit organizations, of special interest to the college-age audience. Briefly covers strategies for those seeking to work internationally.

Jobs for People Who Love to Travel: Opportunities at Home and Abroad—by Ronald Krannich and Carly Rae (Impact Publications, 1999)

Jobs Worldwide—by Davis Lay and Benedict Leerburger (Impact Publications, 1996). Primarily a country-by-country directory of employment opportunities, including names and addresses of international employers

The Overseas Assignment: A Professional's Guide for Working in Developing Countries—by C. N. Weller Jr. (Pennwell Publishers, 1995)

Overseas Summer Jobs—by David Woodworth (Vacation Work, 1999)

Work Abroad: The Complete Guide to Finding a Job Overseas—Susan Griffith and William Nolting, editors (Transitions Abroad Publishing, 1999). Advertisements, articles, and resources for international job seekers. Includes contributions by a variety of authors who have published their works in *Transitions Abroad.*

Work Your Way Around the World—by Susan Griffith (Vacation Work, 1999). Written for British readers, but valuable for anyone seeking work in another country. The book's strength lies in its descriptions of short-term work opportunities abroad and in its country-specific directory. It also includes general information on work permits and travel logistics.

Working in Asia—by Nicki Grihault (Weatherhill, 1996)

S PECIFIC PROFESSIONS OR INDUSTRIES

Accounting Jobs Worldwide—by Tim Ryder (Vacation Work, 1998)

Careers in International Affairs—Maria Pinto Carland, editor (Georgetown University Press, 1996)

Careers in International Business—by Edward J. Halloran (NTC Publishing Group, 1995)

Directory of U.S. Based Agencies Involved in International Health Assistance—(National Council for International Health, 1996). Order directly from the National Council for International Health, 1701 K St. N.W., Suite 600, Washington, DC 20006, 202/833-5900

How to Get a Job with a Cruise Line—by Mary Fallon Miller (Ticket to Adventure, Inc., 1997)

Teaching Abroad: How & Where to Find Teaching & Lecturing Jobs Worldwide—by Roger Jones (How to Books, Ltd., 1998)

Teaching English Abroad: Talk Your Way Around the World!—by Susan Griffith (Vacation Work, 1999)

Working in Hotels & Catering: How to Find Great Employment Opportunities Worldwide—by Mark Hempshell (How to Books, Ltd., 1997)

The World on a String: How to Become a Freelance Foreign Correspondent—Alan Goodman et al, editors (Henry Holt Publishers, 1997)

V OLUNTARY ORGANIZATIONS

Alternatives to the Peace Corps: A Directory of Third World & U.S. Volunteer Opportunities—Filomena Geise, editor (Food First Books, 1999)

International Directory of Volunteer Work—Victoria Pybus, editor (Vacation Work, 1997)

The Peace Corps and More: 175 Ways to Work, Study and Travel at Home and Abroad—by Medea Benjamin and Miya Rodolfo-Sioson (Seven Locks Press, 1997)

INTERNSHIP PROGRAMS

Directory of International Internships: A World of Opportunities—
Charles Gliozzo et al, editors (Michigan State University, 1997). Order
from Career Development and Placement Services, Michigan State
University, 113 Student Services Bldg., East Lansing, MI 48824,
517/355-9510, ext. 371.

*Peterson's Internships 1999: More Than 50,000 Opportunities to Get an
Edge in Today's Competitive Job Market* (Peterson's Guides, 1998)

RELOCATING ABROAD

The Adventures of Working Abroad: Hero Tales from the Global Frontier—
by Joyce Sautters Osland (Jossey Bass Publishers, 1995). Uses Joseph
Campbell's imagery about the hero's journey to describe the lives of
adventurers living and working abroad

*Culture Shock! Successful Living Abroad: Living and Working Abroad—*by
Monica Rabe (Graphic Arts Center Publishing Company, 1997)

*Culture Shock! Successful Living Abroad: A Parent's Guide—*by Robin
Pascoe (Graphic Arts Center Publishing Company, 1999)

*Culture Shock! Successful Living Abroad: A Wife's Guide—*by Robin Pascoe
(Graphic Arts Center Publishing Company, 1993)

*Moving Your Family Overseas—*by Rosalind Kalb and Penelope Welch
(Intercultural Press, Inc., 1992)

*So, You're Going Overseas: A Handbook for Personal and Professional
Success—*by J. Stewart Black and Hal B. Gregersen (Global Business
Publisher, 1998)

*So, You're Going Overseas, Workbook—*by J. Stewart Black and Hal B.
Gregersen (Global Business Publisher, 1998)

*Survival Kit for Overseas Living: For Americans Planning to Live and Work
Abroad—*by L. Robert Kohls (Intercultural Press, Inc., 1996). Pioneering resource for those who want to work internationally. Looks at
stereotypes about Americans and offers practical advice.

*Women's Guide to Overseas Living—*by Nancy J. Piet-Pelon and Barbara
Hornby (Intercultural Press, Inc., 1992)

R EPATRIATION ASSISTANCE

The Art of Coming Home—by Craig Sort (Intercultural Press, 1997)

So, You're Coming Home—by J. Stewart Black and Hal B. Gregersen (Global Business Publisher, 1999)

Strangers at Home: Essays on the Effects of Living Overseas and Coming "Home" to a Strange Land—Carolyn D. Smith, editor (Aletheia Publications, 1996)

H EALTH AND SAFETY FOR INTERNATIONAL TRAVELERS

Bugs, Bites and Bowels—by Dr. Jane Wilson Howarth (Globe Pequot Press, 1995). What a great title!

The Pocket Doctor: A Passport to Healthy Travel—by Stephen Bezruchka (Mountaineers, 1999)

Practical Tips for Americans Travelling Abroad: Ignore Them at Your Own Risk—by Gladson I. Nwanna (World Travel Institute Press, 1998)

Safety and Security for Women Who Travel—by Sheila Suan and Peter Laufer (Travelers' Tales, 1998)

Staying Healthy in Asia, Africa, and Latin America—by Dirk E. Schroeder (Moon Publications, 1999)

I NEXPENSIVE TRAVEL

Air Courier Bargains: How to Travel Worldwide for Next to Nothing— by Kelly Monaghan (Intrepid Traveler, 1998)

Consolidators: Air Travel & Bargain Basement—by Kelly Monaghan (Intrepid Traveler, 1998)

Courier Air Travel Handbook: Learn How to Travel Worldwide for Next to Nothing—by Mark I. Field (Perpetual Press, 1998)

Fly Cheap—by Kelly Monaghan and Rudy Maxa (Intrepid Traveler, 1999)

Fly for Less—by Gary E. Schmidt (Travel Publishing, Inc., 1998)

Worldwide Guide to Cheap Air Fares—by Michael William McColl (Insider Publications, 1998)

CROSS-CULTURAL ETIQUETTE AND BUSINESS COMMUNICATIONS

Chinese Business Etiquette: A Guide to Protocol, Manners and Culture in the People's Republic of China—by Scott D. Seligman and Edward J. Trenn (Warner Books, 1999)

Culturgrams: The Nations Around Us: Africa, Asia and Oceania and *The Americas and Europe*—(David M. Kennedy Center for International Studies, 1998)

Do's and Taboos Around the World—Roger E. Axtell, editor (John Wiley & Sons, 1993)

Do's and Taboos Around the World for Women in Business—by Roger E. Axtell (John Wiley & Sons, 1997)

Do's and Taboos of Humour Around the World—by Roger E. Axtell (John Wiley & Sons, Inc., 1999)

Dun & Bradstreet's Guide to Doing Business Around the World—by Terri Morrison, Wayne A. Conaway, and George A. Borden (Prentice Hall, 1997)

Gestures: The Do's and Taboos of Body Language Around the World—by Roger E. Axtell and Mike Fornwald (John Wiley & Sons, 1998)

Kiss, Bow, or Shake Hands: How to Do Business in 60 Countries—by Terri Morrison, Wayne A. Conaway, and George A. Borden (Adams Media Corporation, 1994)

The International Traveller's Guide to Doing Business in the European Union—by Terri Morrison, Wayne A. Conaway, and George A. Borden (Macmillan General Reference, 1997)

The International Traveller's Guide to Doing Business in Latin America—by Terri Morrison, Wayne A. Conaway, and George A. Borden (Macmillan General Reference, 1997)

Multicultural Manners: New Rules of Etiquette for a Changing Society—by Norine Dresser (John Wiley & Sons, 1996)

There's No Toilet Paper... on the Road Less Traveled: The Best of Travel Humor and Misadventure—Doug Lansky, editor (Travelers' Tales, 1998)

INTERNATIONAL EXECUTIVE RECRUITERS

Directory of Executive Recruiters (Kennedy Publications, 1998)

Executive Recruiters Almanac—Steven Graber, editor (Adams Media Corporation, 1998)

The Global 200 Executive Recruiters: An Essential Guide to the Best Recruiters in the United States, Europe, Asia and Latin America— by Nancy Garrison Jenn (Jossey-Bass Publishers, 1998)

INTERNATIONAL BUSINESS/ TAX INFORMATION

Citizens Working Abroad: Tax Guide 105 (Series 100, Individuals and Families)—by Holmes F. Crouch et al. (All Year Tax Guides, 1998)

The Expat's Guide to U.S. Taxes (Hands on Help for Americans Overseas)—by Jane A. Bruno (Bruno Expat Tax Services, 1998)

Tax Guide for U.S. Citizens Abroad (Publication 54). Order from Forms Distribution Center, P.O. Box 25866, Richmond, VA 23260

INTERNATIONAL BUSINESS DIRECTORIES

Directory of American Firms Operating in Foreign Countries (World Trade Academy Press, 1999)

Directory of Foreign Firms Operating in the United States (World Trade Academy Press, 1998)

Encyclopedia of Global Industries (Gale Research, 1999)

Major Companies of Central & Eastern Europe and the Commonwealth of Independent States (Gale Research, 1999)

N ATIONAL AND INTERNATIONAL ASSOCIATIONS

Encyclopedia of Associations (Gale Research, 1999)

National Trade and Professional Associations of the United States (Columbia Books, Inc., 1998)

Yearbook of International Organizations (Union of International Associations, 1999)

I NTERNATIONAL TRAVEL PUBLICATIONS

International Travel News—1901 Royal Oaks Dr., Suite 190, Sacramento, CA 95815, 800/486-4968

Rick Steves' Europe Travel Newsletter—120 Fourth Ave. N., P.O. Box 2009, Edmonds, WA 98020, 425/771-8303, www.ricksteves.com

Transitions Abroad, The Guide to Learning, Living and Working Overseas—P.O. Box 1300, Amherst, MA 01004, 800/293-0373, www.transabroad.com

S UBSCRIPTION PUBLICATIONS LISTING INTERNATIONAL JOBS

Current Jobs International—P.O. Box 40550, Washington, DC 20016, 703/506-4400

Global Alternatives—Professional Development Resource Center, School for International Training, Box 676, Kipling Rd., Brattleboro, VT 05302, 802/258-3397, fax 802/258-3248

International Employment Gazette—220 N. Main St., Suite 100, Greenville, SC 29601, 800/882-9188, fax 803/235-3369

International Employment Hotline—Worldwise Books, P.O. Box 3030, Oakton, VA 22124, 703/620-1972, fax 703/620-1973

TESOL Placement Bulletin—1600 Cameron St., #300, Alexandria, VA 22314, 703/836-0744, fax 703/836-7864

N EWSPAPERS AND MAGAZINES LISTING INTERNATIONAL JOBS

The Economist—P.O. Box 14, Harold Hall, Romford, Essex RM3 8EQ;
   gca@economist.com

Financial Times—14 E. 60th St., New York, NY 10022, 800/628-8088.

International Herald Tribune—850 Third Ave., Eighth Floor, New York,
   NY 10022, 800/882-2884

New York Times—229 W. 43rd St., New York, NY 10036, 212/353-8700

World Press Review—700 Broadway, New York, NY 10003, 212/982-8880

Appendix B

Internet Resources

Worldwide Employment Sites

Asia-Net, www.asia-net.com
Of particular interest to bilingual professionals who speak English and Japanese, Chinese, or Korean.

Australia, www.employment.com.au
Lists employment opportunities in Australia by employer and by consultant. Also accessible through Career Mosaic's International Gateway.

Career Center, www.netline.com/career
Provides links to employment sites such as Career Mosaic, Career Path, and Job Trak. Includes international listings, resume and recruitment information, and job listings for recent graduates.

Career Mosaic, www.careermosaic.com
Primarily lists jobs in the United States, but you can enter the International Gateway to check out international sites by geographical location, a jobs database, and employer profiles.

Career Resource Center, www.careers.org
Links to numerous sites, including Career Mosaic and Monster Board, but you'll have to sift through the sites for international employment opportunities.

Campus Review: International Academic Job Market
www.camrev.com.au/share/jobs.html
Employment listings in such fields as education, health and medicine, engineering, law, and more.

International Employment Opportunities
http://members.iquest.net/~swlodin/jobs/overseas.html
Links to sites featuring international employment opportunities and resources.

International Job and Volunteer Sites
www.urich.edu/~worldoie/jobs.htm
From the office of international education at the University of Richmond. Links to graduate programs in international studies, international job sites, and general resources.

International Job Centers
www.jerryeden.com/ijc/joblist.htm
Lists 1,500,000 jobs and charges a $10 registration fee.

Jobspace: The European Space for Jobs
www.jobspace.com
Listings for jobs in Europe, specifically Belgium, France, and Germany.

Monster Board, www.monster.com
While not exclusive to the overseas job market, Monster Board does provide links to more than 2,000 job listings around the world in such locations as Africa, Asia, Europe, Mexico, the Middle East, and South America.

Overseas Job Express, www.overseasjobs.com
Focusing on the global job market, this site offers more than 40 categories of international jobs, international listings, sample news articles, job search resources, a guide to embassies around the world, and links to other sites of interest to expatriates.

University of San Francisco
www.usfca.edu/career/international.html
A collection of sites with international employment information, organized by general/global resources and by regions worldwide.

World-Wide Web Employment Office
www.harbornet.com/biz/office/annex.html
Lists international employment opportunities by occupation rather than industry. The site's International Employers Directory provides access to more than 600 occupational categories, with links to countries around the world.

JOBS WITH THE U.S. GOVERNMENT

U.S. Office of Personnel Management
www.opm.gov
This site provides thorough information about applying for domestic and international jobs with the federal government. For working abroad, you'll find information about qualifications, salary, the application process, and appointments for employees returning from overseas assignments.

U.S. State Department-Bureau of Consular Affairs
http://travel.state.gov
Check the section on career opportunities and you'll find subsections on International Vacancy Announcements and International Organizations' Addresses and Employment Web Sites. Listed positions are generally for operations, administrative, and technical officers with advanced degrees, 12 to 20 years of related job experience, and fluency in at least one foreign language.

VOLUNTEER OPPORTUNITIES ABROAD

Global Service Corps, www.globalservicecorps.org
Global Service Corps places adults in short- and long-term volunteer projects in developing nations around the world.

Peace Corps, www.peacecorps.gov
Information on applying for "the toughest job you'll ever love." The site includes news, volunteer stories, volunteer opportunities by industry and region, global education information, and a great kids' section.

CLASSIFIED ADS

Career Path, www.careerpath.com
Includes daily classified ads from more than 60 American newspapers.

American Journalism Review Newslink
www.newslink.org/news.html
The site highlights about 5,000 newspapers worldwide and 30 of the top magazines in the United States and Canada.

Editor and Publisher Interactive
www.mediainfo.com
At this site, you can gain access to more than 100 top newspapers and their employment listings. The site also gives you access to other media, such as magazines, TV, and radio.

National Ad Search
www.nationaladsearch.com
Displays ads from more than 60 major American newspapers. A usage fee is required; order a one-week trial subscription and a sample printed issue before subscribing.

COMPANY INFORMATION

Europages, the European Business Directory
www.europages.com

Lists 500,000 companies, with names and addresses, in 30 countries. You can search for information by product or service, industry, or company name.

Companies Online, www.companiesonline.com

Provides information on more than 100,000 public and private companies, as well as business associations and professional organizations.

Gale Group, www.gale.com

Allows you to research the Gale Group's list of publications, including its *Directory of Multinationals*, *Major Companies of Europe*, and *National Directory of Non-Profit Organizations*. Note that the directories themselves are costly and are generally available at libraries.

Deloitte & Touche's Peerscape
www.peerscape.com

A database of more than 19,000 companies in 49 countries.

Hoover's Online, www.hoovers.com

An excellent resource and by far my favorite for researching company information. You can receive general information for free from its Company Capsules service or pay a fee to generate your own lists of companies by location and industry. Click on "Lists" to explore a variety of top companies in different categories. The site also provides links to sites like Career Mosaic, Monster Board, and the *Wall Street Journal*.

American City Business Journals, www.amcity.com

The site provides access to business journals in major American metropolitan areas. You can scan the headlines of recent issues and get more detailed company and industry information from lead articles and weekly features.

S EARCH AND EMPLOYMENT AGENCIES

Jobsite, www.jobsite.co.uk/home/abroad.html

Lists leading European recruitment agencies and employers with links to sites in Europe, the Middle East, and the United States. Services include job listings via e-mail, resume postings, and advice on resume and CV writing.

Handilinks, www.ahandyguide.com/cat1/employ.htm

A directory that allows you to research various employment areas, including employment agencies and executive search firms. Includes information on internships and job fairs.

Headhunter.Net, www.headhunter.net/

The top five industries represented at this site are information technology, engineering, accounting, sales, and marketing, with salary ranges between $51,000 and $100,000.

International Career Information, Inc., www.rici.com

A recruiting company with links to InterCareer Net for Japanese-English bilingual business and information technology professionals and to Inter-Career Net Japan for bilingual students and recent graduates.

C ULTURAL AND GEOGRAPHICAL INFORMATION

America Online International Channel

A good place to start when you want to learn about the culture of another country. You can access international business and social etiquette information, hear the latest world news, look through international newspapers, enter chat rooms with individuals from around the world, post questions, and research news information.

Argus Clearinghouse, www.clearinghouse.net
Provides a list of telephone directories on the Web, with links to Yellow Pages and business directories.

Citynet, www.city.net
This site can connect you to Web sites about more than 5,000 locations around the world.

Free Real Audio, http://freeyellow.com/members3/rgh/index.html
This site allows you to listen in on live radio broadcasts from around the world, in both English and foreign languages.

ORGANIZATIONS FOR AMERICANS ABROAD

American Citizens Abroad (ACA), www.aca.ch
This nonprofit organization, dedicated to serving and defending the interests of U.S. citizens around the world, offers a potpourri of news items and links to newspapers, radio stations, and other sites of interest to expatriates.

Association of American Residents Overseas (AARO) http://members.aol.com/aaroparis/aarohome.htm
The organization works to protect the rights of American citizens abroad through its newsletter, seminars, forums, and voting rallies. The group also offers overseas medical insurance plans to members.

Embassy Page www.embpage.org or www.embassyweb.com
A valuable resource for anyone traveling abroad, with links to diplomatic offices, international sites, world news, an open forum, a global bookstore, and an archive of e-mailed questions from visitors with answers provided by embassy staff.

Embassy World, www.embassyworld.com
Includes a searchable database for every embassy and consulate office in the world.

Escape Artist, www.escapeartist.com
Information on living, working, investing, and traveling abroad, with links to magazines featuring articles about the overseas experience. Country destination profiles and international reference pages are also available.

Expat Access, www.expataccess.com/
A valuable resource for expats in Europe. The site includes tips on moving to and living in specific European countries, with information on international schools, working spouses, and culture shock. Discussion boards and free classified ads are also available.

Expat Exchange, www.expatexchange.com
A resource for expats offering advice from experts, a chat room, and links to international employment information and classified listings.

Expat Forum, www.expatforum.com
Includes tidbits of information on the cost of living, electricity and appliances, and telephone service abroad. Also offers articles, an HR forum, and chat rooms for 24 country-specific areas.

Living Abroad, www.livingabroad.com
Offers help with relocation, international school listings, 81 country profiles, and valuable links for international business travelers and expats in general.

Overseas Digest, http://overseasdigest.com
The sister site of Expat Exchange, Overseas Digest offers a free newsletter, reports on living abroad, and an extensive bookstore. Gives 26 vital government documents of interest to expats, including the *Tips for Travelers Series* to country-specific destinations.

INDUSTRY-SPECIFIC SITES

Hospitality Net Virtual Job Exchange
www.hospitalitynet.nl/job
Provides industry news, forums, and a bookshelf of industry-specific literature for those interested in the hospitality industry. The job exchange features seasonal listings as well as long-term employment opportunities.

Job Serve, www.jobserve.com
Technology job listings from around the world.

Search Associates, www.search-associates.com
An international placement organization for teachers and administrators.

WW Teach
http://members.aol.com/wwteach/Teach.htm
An educational resource for international teachers. Includes information on and links to international schools and associations, teaching positions, travel, overseas living resources, educational conferences, cultural guides, and tips for saving money while overseas. Updated infrequently.

GENERAL TRAVEL INFORMATION

Centers for Disease Control
www.cdc.gov/travel/travel.html
Provides updates on disease outbreaks around the world, geographic health recommendations, and reference materials for international travelers.

International Association for Medical Assistance to Travelers, www.sentex.net/~iamat

Nonprofit foundation that advises travelers about health risks and immunization requirements for specific geographical regions. Helps travelers locate competent English-speaking doctors and hospitals around the world.

Travlang's Foreign Language for Travelers www.travlang.com/languages

A great resource for travelers and anyone who wants to learn one of more than 70 foreign languages. Includes information on exchange rates and currency, translating dictionaries, and a word of the day.

Appendix C
American Chambers of Commerce Abroad

ARGENTINA
Leandro N. Alem 1110, Piso 13
1001 Buenos Aires
[54] (1) 331-5420 5126

AUSTRALIA
Level 1, 300 Flinders St.
Adelaide, South Australia 5000
[61] (8) 224-0761
Level 2, 41 Lower Fort St.
Sydney, New South Wales 2000
[61] (2) 241-1907
Level 1, 123 Lonsdale St.
Melbourne, Victoria 3000
[61] (3) 663-2644
Level 23, 68 Queen St.
Brisbane, Queensland 4000
[61] (7) 221-8542
Level 6, 231 Adelaide Terrace
Perth, Western Australia 6000
[61] (9) 325-9540

AUSTRIA
Porzellangasse 35
1090 Vienna
[43] (1) 319-5751

BELGIUM
Avenue des Arts 50, Boite 5
1040, Brussels
[32] (2) 513-6770/9

BOLIVIA
Casilla 8268
Avda. Area No. 20171
Ofieina 3, La Paz
[591] (2) 342-523

BRAZIL
C.P 916, Praca Pio X-15
Fifth Floor
20040 Rio de Janeiro, RJ
[55| (21) 203-2477
Rua da Espanha 2
Salas 604-606
40000 Salvador, Bahia
[55] (71) 242-0077; 5606
Rua Alexandre Dumas 1976
04717 Sao Paulo, SP,
[55] (11) 246-9199

CHILE
Ave. Amerigo Vespucio Sur 80
9 Pisco, 82 Correo 34
Santiago
[56] (2) 208-4140; 3451

CHINA
Great Wall Sheraton Hotel
Room 301, N. Donghuan Ave.
Beijing 100026
[86] (1) 500-5566 ext. 2271
Shanghai Centre, Room 435
1376 Nanjing Rd. W.
Shanghai 200040
[86] (21) 279-7119

COLOMBIA
Apdo. Aereo 8008
Transversal 19, #12263, Bogota
[57] (1) 215-8859
Avenida 1N, No. 3N-97, Cali
[57] (23) 610-162; 572-993
Centro Comercial Bocagrande
Avda. San Martin, Of. 309
P.O. Box 15555, Cartagena
[57] (53) 657-724
Centro Colombo American,
Apdo. Aereo 734, Medellin
[57] (4) 513-4444

COSTA RICA
c/o Aerocasillas, P.O. Box 025216
Dept. 1526, Miami, FL 33102
506/220-2200

CZECH REPUBLIC
Karlovo namestf 24
110 00 Prague 1
[42] (2) 299-887; 296-778

DOMINICAN REPUBLIC
American Chamber EPS #A-528
P.O. Box 02-5256
Miami, FL 33102
809/544-2222

ECUADOR
Av. Cevallos y Montalvo
3er. Piso, Oficina 301, Ambato
[593] (2) 821-073
Avda. Octavio Chacon 1-55
Centro Comercial de Parque
Industrial, 2do Piso, Oficina 303
Casilla 01.01.0534, Cuenca
[593] (7) 861-873
Edificio Banco del Pichincha
Manta, [593] (4) 621-699
Edificio Multicentro, 4P, La Nina y
Avda. 6 de Diciembre, Quito
[593] (2) 507-450

EGYPT
Cairo Marriott Hotel, Suite 1541
P.O. Box 33, Zamalek, Cairo
[20] (2) 340-8888

EL SALVADOR
87 Avenida Norte, No. 720, Apt. A
Col. Escalon, San Salvador
[503] 223-3292

GERMANY
Rossmarkt 12, Postfach 100 162
60311 Frankfurt am Main 1
[49] (69) 28-34-01
Budapesterstrasse 29, W-1000
Berlin 30
[49] (30) 261-55-86

GREECE
16 Kanari St., Third Floor
Athens 106 74
[30] (1) 36-18-385; 36-36-407

GUAM
102 Ada Plaza Center
P.O. Box 283, Agana, 96910
[671] 472-6311; 8001

GUATEMALA
6a Avenida 14-77, Zona 10
Guatemala City 01010
[502] (2) 374-489; 683-106

HONDURAS
Hotel Honduras Maya
Ap. Pos. 1838, Tegucigalpa
[504] 32-70-43
Centro Bella Aurora, 6 Avenida
13-14 Calles, N.O., San Pedro Sula
[504] 58-0164

HONG KONG
1030 Swire House, Chater Rd.
[852] 526-0165

HUNGARY
Dozsa Gyorgy ut. 84/A
Room 222, 1068 Budapest
[36] (1) 142-7518

INDIA
Mohan Development Bldg.
11th Floor, 13, Tolstoy Marg
New Delhi 110 001
[91] (11) 332-2723

INDONESIA
Landmark Centre
22nd Floor, Suite 2204
Jl. Jendral Sudirman, Jakarta
[62] (21) 571-0800 ext. 2222

IRELAND
20 College Green, Dublin 2
[353] (1) 679-3733

ISRAEL
35 Shaul Hamelech Blvd.
64927 Tel Aviv
[972] (3) 695-2341

ITALY
Via Cantu 1, 20123 Milano
[39] (2) 86-90-661

IVORY COAST
01 BP 3394, Abidjan 01
[225] 21-46-16

JAMAICA
Wyndham Hotel
77 Knutsford Blvd., Kingston 5
(809) 926-7866

JAPAN
Bridgestone Toranomon Bldg.
Fifth Floor
3-25-2 Toranomon
Minato-ku, Tokyo 105
[81] (3) 3433-5381
P.O. Box 235
Okinawa City 904
[81] (9) 889-8935-2684

KOREA
Room 307, Chosun Hotel, Seoul
[82] (2) 753-6471; 6516

LATVIA
Jauniela 24, Room 205, Riga
[371] (2) 215-205

MALAYSIA
15.01 Lev 15th Fl., Amoda
22 Jalan Imbi
55100 Kuala Lumpur
[60] (3) 248-2407; 2540

MEXICO
P.O. Box 60326, Apdo. 113
Houston, TX 77205
[52] (57) 24-3800
Avda. Moctezuma #442
Col. Jardines del Sol
45050 Zapopan, Jalisco
[52] (36) 34-6606

Rio Orinoco 307 Ote.
Col. del Valle, San Pedro Garza
Garcia, Nuevo Leon
[52] (8) 335-6210

MOROCCO
18, Rue Colbert
Casablanca 01
[212] (2) 31-14 48

NETHERLANDS
Carnegieplein 5, 2517 KJ
the Hague
[31] (70) 3-65-98-08

NEW ZEALAND
P.O. Box 106-002
Auckland 1001
[64] (9) 309-9140

NICARAGUA
Apdo. 202, Managua
[505] (2) 67-30-99

PAKISTAN
NIC Building, Sixth Floor
Abbasi Shaheed Rd.
G.P.O. Box 1322, Karachi 74000
[92] (21) 526-436

PANAMA
Apdo.168, Estafeta Balboa
Panama City
[507] 69-3881

PARAGUAY
Edif. El Faro International Piso 4
Asuncion
[595] (21) 442-135/6

PERU
Av. Ricardo Palma 836
Miraflores, Lima 18
[51] (14) 47 9349

PHILIPPINES
P.O. Box 1578, MCC
Manila,
[63] (2) 818-7911

POLAND
Swietokrzyska 36 m 6
Entrance 1, 00-116 Warsaw
[48] (22) 209-867 ext. 222

PORTUGAL
Rua de D. Estefania, 155, 5 Esq.
Lisbon P-1000
[351] (1) 57 25 61

ROMANIA
Str. Gh. Manu nr. 9
71-106 Bucharest 1
[40] (1) 659-3600 ext. 127

SAUDI ARABIA
P.O. Box 88
Dhahran Airport 31932
[966] (3) 857-6464
Hyatt Regency-Jeddah
P.O. Box 8483, Jeddah 21482
[966] (2) 652-1234 ext. 1759

P.O. Box 3050
Riyadh 11471, 07045
[966] (1) 477-7341

SINGAPORE
1 Scotts Rd., 16-07 Shaw Center
0922, [65] 235-0077

SOUTH AFRICA
P 0. Box 1132, 60 Fifth St.
Lower Houghton
2196 Johannesburg
[27] (11) 788-0265/6

SPAIN
Avda. Diagonal 477
08036 Barcelona
[34] (3) 405-1266
Hotel EuroBuilding
Padre Damian 23, 28036 Madrid
[34] (1) 458-6559

SRI LANKA
P.O. Box 1000, Lotus Rd.
Colombo Hilton, Third Floor
Colombo 1
[94] (1) 54-4644 ext. 2318

SWEDEN
Box 5512, 114 85 Stockholm
[46] (8) 666-11-00

SWITZERLAND
Talacker 41, 8001 Zurich
[41] (1) 211-24-54

TAIWAN

123-3, Ta-Pei Rd.
First Floor, #1-1
Niao Sung Hsiang
Kaohsiung County 83305
[886] (7) 731-3712
Room 1012, Chia Hsin Bldg.
Annex, 96 Chung Shan N. Rd.
Section 2, Taipei
[886] (2) 581-7089

THAILAND

P.O. Box 1095
140 Wireless Rd., Seventh Floor
Kian Gwan Building, Bangkok
[66] (2) 251-9266

TRINIDAD
AND TOBAGO

Hilton International
Upper Arcade, Lady Young Rd.
Port of Spain
(809) 627-8570

TURKEY

Altay Is Merkezi 601
Sair Esref Bulvari No. 18
Izmir 35250
[90] (51) 41-40-68/70
Fahri Gizdem Sokak 22/5
80280 Gayrettepe, Istanbul
[90] (1) 274-2824; 288-6212

UKRAINE

7 Kudriavsky Uzviv
Second Floor
Kiev 252053
[7] (044) 417-1015

UNITED ARAB
EMIRATES

International Trade Center
Suite 1610
P.O. Box 9281, Dubai
[971] (4) 314-735

UNITED KINGDOM

75 Brook St.
London WIY 2EB
[44] (71) 493-03-81

URUGUAY

Calle Bartolome Mitre 1337
Cassilla de Correo 809
Montevideo
[598] (2) 9-590-59/48

VENEZUELA

Torre Credival, Piso 10, 2da.
Avenida de Campo Alegre
Campo Alegre, Apdo. 5181
Campo, Caracas 1010-A

Appendix D

Foreign Embassies in the United States

Call before you fax for information.

ALBANIA
Embassy of the
Republic of Albania, 2100 S St. N.W.
Washington, DC 20008
202/223-4942, fax 202/628-7342

ALGERIA
Embassy of the Democratic and
Popular Republic of Algeria
2118 Kalorama Rd. N.W.
Washington DC 20008
202/265-2800, fax 202/667-2174

ANGOLA
Embassy of the Republic of Angola
1615 M St. N.W. Suite 900
Washington, DC 20036
202/785-1156, fax 202/785-1258

ANTIGUA AND BARBUDA
Embassy of Antigua and Barbuda
3216 New Mexico Ave. N.W.
Washington, DC 20016
202/362-5211, fax 202/362-5225

ARGENTINA
Embassy of the Argentine Republic
1600 New Hampshire Ave. N.W.
Washington, DC 20009
202/238-6400, fax 202/238-6471

ARMENIA
Embassy of the
Republic of Armenia
2225 R St. N.W.
Washington, DC 20008
202/319-1976, fax 202/319-2982

AUSTRALIA
Embassy of Australia,
1601 Massachusetts Ave. N.W.
Washington, DC 20036
202/797-3000, fax 202/797-3168

AUSTRIA
Embassy of Austria,
3524 International Court N.W.
Washington, DC 20008
202/895-6700, fax 202/895-6750

AZERBAIJAN
Embassy of the Republic of
Azerbaijan (temporary)
927 15th St. N.W. #700
Washington, DC 20005
202/842-0001, fax 202/842-0004

BAHAMAS
Embassy of the
Commonwealth of the Bahamas
2220 Massachusetts Ave. N.W.
Washington, DC 20008
202/319-2660, fax 202/319-2668

BAHRAIN
Embassy of the State of Bahrain
3502 International Dr. N.W.
Washington, DC 20008
202/342-0741, fax 202/362-2192

BANGLADESH
Embassy of the People's Republic
of Bangladesh
2201 Wisconsin Ave. N.W.
Washington, DC 20007
202/342-8372

BARBADOS
Embassy of Barbados
2144 Wyoming Ave. N.W.
Washington, DC 20008
202/939-9200

BELARUS
Embassy of the
Republic of Belarus
1619 New Hampshire Ave. N.W.
Washington, DC 20009
202/986-1604, fax 202/986-1805

BELGIUM
Embassy of Belgium
3330 Garfield St. N.W.
Washington, DC 20008
202/333-6900, fax 202/333-3079

BELIZE
Embassy of Belize
2535 Massachusetts Ave. N.W.
Washington, DC 20008
202/332-9636, fax 202/332-6888

BENIN
Embassy of the People's
Republic of Benin
2737 Cathedral Ave. N.W.
Washington, DC 20008
202/232-6656, fax 202/0265-1996

BOLIVIA
Embassy of Bolivia
3014 Massachusetts Ave. N.W.
Washington, DC 20008
202/483-4410, fax 202/328-3712

BOSNIA-HERZEGOVINA
Embassy of Bosnia-Herzegovina
1707 L St. N.W. #760
Washington DC 20036
202/833-3612 , fax 202/833-2061

BOTSWANA
Embassy of Botswana
3400 International Dr. N.W.
Washington, DC 20008
202/244-4990, fax 202/244-4164

BRAZIL
Embassy of Brazil
3006 Massachusetts Ave. N.W.
Washington, DC 20008
202/238-2700, fax 202/238-2827

BRUNEI
Embassy of Brunei Darussalm
2600 Virginia Ave. N.W. #300
Washington, DC 20037
202/342-0159, fax 202/342-0158

BULGARIA
Embassy of Bulgaria
1621 22nd St. N.W.
Washington, DC 20008
202/387-7969, fax 202/234-7973

BURKINA FASO
Embassy of Burkina Faso,
2340 Massachusetts Ave. N.W.
Washington, DC 20008
202/332-5577

BURMA (see Myanmar)

BURUNDI
Embassy of Burundi
2233 Wisconsin Ave. N.W. #212
Washington, DC 20007
202/342-2574, fax 202/342-2578

CAMBODIA
Embassy of Cambodia
4500 16th St. N.W.
Washington, DC 20011
202/726-7742, fax 202/726-8381

CAMEROON
Embassy of the United
Republic of Cameroon
2349 Massachusetts Ave. N.W.
Washington, DC 20008
202/265-8790

CANADA
Embassy of Canada
501 Pennsylvania Ave. N.W.
Washington, DC 20001
202/682-1740, fax 202/682-7726

CAPE VERDE
Embassy of Cape Verde 3
415 Massachusetts Ave. N.W.
Washington, DC 20007
202/965-6820, fax 202/965-1207

CENTRAL AFRICAN REPUBLIC
Embassy of the
Central African Republic
1618 22nd St. N.W.
Washington, DC 20008
202/483-7800, fax 202/332-9893

CHAD
Embassy of Chad
2002 R St. N.W.
Washington, DC 20009
202/462-4009, fax 202/265-1937

CHILE
Embassy of Chile
1732 Massachusetts Ave. N.W.
Washington, DC 20036
202/785-1746, fax 202/887-5579

CHINA
Embassy of the People's
Republic of China
2300 Connecticut Ave. N.W.
Washington, DC 20008
202/328-2500

COLOMBIA
Embassy of Colombia
2118 Leroy Pl. N.W.
Washington, DC 20008
202/387-8338, fax 202/232-8643

COMOROS
Embassy of Comoros,UN Mission
336 E. 45th St., Second Floor
New York, NY 10017
212/972-8010, fax 212/983-4712

CONGO (Zaire)
Embassy of the Democratic
Republic of the Congo
1800 New Hampshire Ave. N.W.
Washington, DC 20009
202/234-7690, fax 202/237-0748

CONGO, REPUBLIC OF
Embassy of the
Republic of the Congo
4891 Colorado Ave. N.W.
Washington, DC 20011
202/726-0825, fax 202/265-4795

COSTA RICA
Embassy of Costa Rica
2114 S St. N.W.
Washington, DC 20008
202/234-2945, fax 202/265-4795

COTE D'IVOIRE
Embassy of the Cote d'Ivoire
2424 Massachusetts Ave. N.W.
Washington, DC 20008
202/797-0300

CROATIA
Embassy of Croatia
2343 Massachusetts Ave. N.W.
Washington, DC 20008
202/588-5899, fax 202/588-8936

CYPRUS
Embassy of Cyprus
2211 R St. N.W.
Washington, DC 20008
202/462-5772, fax 202/483-6710

CZECH REPUBLIC
Embassy of the Czech Republic
3900 Spring of Freedom St. N.W.
Washington, DC 20008
202/274-9100, fax 202/966-8540

DENMARK
Royal Danish Embassy, Chancery
3200 Whitehaven St. N.W.
Washington, DC 20008
202/234-4300, fax 202/328-1470

DJIBOUTI
Embassy of the
Republic of Djibouti
1156 15th St. N.W., Suite 515
Washington, DC 20005
202/331-0270, fax 202/331-0302

DOMINICA
Embassy of the
Commonwealth of Dominica
3216 New Mexico Ave. N.W.
Washington, DC 20016
202/364-6781, fax 202/364-6791

DOMINICAN REPUBLIC
Embassy of the
Dominican Republic
1715 22nd St. N.W.
Washington, DC 20008
202/332-6280, fax 202/265-8057

ECUADOR
Embassy of Ecuador
2535 15th St. N.W.,
Washington, DC 20009
202/234-7200, fax 202/667-3482

EGYPT
Embassy of the Arab
Republic of Egypt
3521 International Court N.W.
Washington, DC 20008
202/895-5400, fax 202/244-4319

EL SALVADOR
Embassy of El Salvador
2308 California St. N.W.
Washington, DC 20008
202/265-9671

EQUATORIAL GUINEA
Embassy of the
Republic of Equatorial Guinea
1712 I St. N.W., Suite 410
Washington, DC 20006
202/296-4174, fax 202/296-4195

ERITREA
Embassy of Eritrea
1708 New Hampshire Ave. N.W.
Washington, DC 20009
202/319-1991, fax 202/393-0348

ESTONIA
Embassy of Estonia
2131 Massachusetts Ave. N.W.
Washington, DC 20008
202/588-0101, fax 202/588-0108

ETHIOPIA
Embassy of Ethiopia
2134 Kalorama Rd. N.W.
Washington, DC 20008
202/234-2281, fax 202/328-7950

FIJI
Embassy of Fiji
2233 Wisconsin Ave. N.W., #240
Washington, DC 20007
202/337-8320, fax 202/337-1996

FINLAND
Embassy of Finland
3301 Massachusetts Ave. N.W.
Washington, DC 20008
202/298-5800, fax 202/298-6030

FRANCE
Embassy of France
4101 Reservoir Rd. N.W.
Washington, DC 20007
202/944-6000, fax 202/944-6166

GABON
Embassy of the
Republic of Gabon,
2034 20th St. N.W. #200
Washington, DC 20009
202/797-1000, fax 202/332-0668

GAMBIA
Embassy of Gambia
1155 15th St. N.W. #1000
Washington, DC 20009
202/785-1399, fax 202/785-1430

GEORGIA
Embassy of Georgia
1511 K St. N.W. #424
Washington, DC 20005
202/393-5959, fax 202/393-6060

GERMANY
Embassy of German
Federal Republic
4645 Reservoir Rd. N.W.
Washington, DC 20007
202/298-4000, fax 202/298-4249

GHANA
Embassy of Ghana
3512 International Dr. N.W.
Washington, DC 20008
202/686-4520, fax 202/686-4527

GREECE
Embassy of Greece
2221 Massachusetts Ave. N.W.
Washington, DC 20008
202/939-5800, fax 202/939-5824

GRENADA
Embassy of Grenada
1701 New Hampshire Ave. N.W.
Washington, DC 20009
202/265-2561

GUATEMALA
Embassy of Guatemala
2220 R St. N.W.
Washington, DC 20008
202/745-4952, fax 202/745-1908

GUINEA
Embassy of Guinea
2112 Leroy Pl. N.W.
Washington, DC 20008
202/483-9420, fax 202/483-8688

GUINEA-BISSAU
Embassy of Guinea-Bissau
1511 K St. N.W. #519
Washington, DC 20005
202/347-3950, fax 202/347-3954

GUYANA
Embassy of Guyana
2490 Tracy Pl. N.W.
Washington, DC 20008
202/265-6900

HAITI
Embassy of Haiti
2311 Massachusetts Ave. N.W.
Washington, DC 20008
202/332-4090, fax 202/745-7215

HOLY SEE
Embassy of the Holy See
3339 Massachusetts Ave. N.W.
Washington, DC 20008
202/333-7121

HONDURAS
Embassy of Honduras
3007 Tilden St. N.W.
Washington, DC 20008
202/966-7702, fax 202/966-9751

HUNGARY
Embassy of Hungary
3910 Shoemaker St. N.W.
Washington, DC 20008
202/362-6730, fax 202/966-8135

ICELAND
Embassy of Iceland
1156 15th St. N.W. #1200
Washington, DC 20005
202/265-6653, fax 202/265-6656

INDIA
Embassy of India
2107 Massachusetts Ave. N.W.
Washington, DC 20008
202/939-7000, fax 202/483-3972

INDONESIA
Embassy of Indonesia
2020 Massachusetts Ave. N.W.
Washington, DC 20008
202/775-5200, fax 202/775-5365

IRELAND
Embassy of Ireland
2234 Massachusetts Ave. N.W.
Washington, DC 20008
202/462 3939, fax 202/232-5993

ISRAEL
Embassy of Israel
3514 International Dr. N.W.
Washington, DC 20008
202/364-5500, fax 202/364-5610

ITALY
Embassy of Italy
1601 Fuller St. N.W.
Washington, DC 20009
202/328-5500, fax 202/483-2187

JAMAICA
Embassy of Jamaica
1520 New Hampshire Ave. N.W.
Washington, DC 20036
202/452-0660, fax 202/452-0081

JAPAN
Embassy of Japan
2520 Massachusetts Ave. N.W.
Washington, DC 20008
202/238-6700, fax 202/328-2187

JORDAN
Embassy of Jordan
3504 International Dr. N.W.
Washington, DC 20008
202/966-2664, fax 202/966-3110

KAZAKHSTAN
Embassy of the
Republic of Kazakhstan
1401 16th St., N.W.
Washington, DC 20036
202/232-5488, fax 202/232-5845

KENYA
Embassy of the Republic of Kenya
2249 R St. N.W.
Washington, DC 20008
202/387-6101, fax 202/462-3829

KOREA
Embassy of the
Republic of South Korea
2450 Massachusetts Ave. N.W.
Washington, DC 20008
202/939-5600, fax 202/387-0205

KUWAIT
Embassy of the State of Kuwait
2940 Tilden St. N.W.
Washington, DC 20008
202/966-0702, fax 202/966-0517

KYRGYZSTAN
Embassy of Kyrgyzstan
1732 Wisconsin Ave. N.W.
Washington, DC 20007
202/338-5141, fax 202/338-5139

LAOS
Embassy of the Lao People's
Democratic Republic
2222 S St. N.W.
Washington, DC 20008
202/332-6416, fax 202/332-4923

LATVIA
Embassy of Latvia
4325 17th St. N.W.
Washington, DC 20011
202/726-8213, fax 202/726-6785

LEBANON
Embassy of Lebanon
2560 28th St. N.W.
Washington, DC 20008
202/939-6300, fax 202/939-6324

LESOTHO
Embassy of Lesotho
2511 Massachusetts Ave. N.W.
Washington, DC 20008
202/797-5533, fax 202/234-6815

LIBERIA
Embassy of Liberia
5201 16th St. N.W.
Washington, DC 20011
202/723-0437

LITHUANIA
Embassy of Lithuania
2622 16th St. N.W.
Washington, DC 20009
202/234-5860, fax 202/328-0466

LUXEMBOURG
Embassy of Luxembourg
2200 Massachusetts Ave. N.W.
Washington, DC 20008
202/234-5860, fax 202/328-0466

MACEDONIA
Embassy of Macedonia
3050 K St. N.W. #210
Washington, DC 20007
202/337-3063, fax 202/337-3093

MADAGASCAR
Embassy of Madagascar
2374 Massachusetts Ave. N.W.
Washington, DC 20008
202/265-5525

MALAWI
Embassy of Malawi
2408 Massachusetts Ave. N.W.
Washington, DC 20008
202/797-1007

MALAYSIA
Embassy of Malaysia
2401 Massachusetts Ave. N.W.
Washington, DC 20008
202/328-2700, fax 202/483-7661

MALDIVES
Embassy of Maldives, UN Mission
820 Second Ave. #800C
New York, NY 10017
212/599-6195, fax 212/661-6405

MALI
Embassy of the Republic of Mali
2130 R St. N.W.
Washington, DC 20008
202/332-2249, fax 202/332-6603

MALTA
Embassy of Malta
2017 Connecticut Ave. N.W.
Washington, DC 20008
202/462-3611, fax 202/387-5470

MARSHALL ISLANDS
Embassy of the Marshall Islands
2433 Massachusetts Ave. N.W.
Washington, DC 20008
202/234-5414, fax 202/232-3236

MAURITANIA
Embassy of Mauritania
2129 Leroy Pl. N.W.
Washington, DC 20008
202/232-5700, fax 202/319-2623

MAURITIUS
Embassy of Mauritius
4301 Connecticut Ave. N.W. #441
Washington, DC 20008
202/244-1491, fax 202/966-0983

MEXICO
Embassy of Mexico
1911 Pennsylvania Ave. N.W.
Washington, DC 20006
202/728-1600, fax 202/728-1698

MICRONESIA
Embassy of Micronesia
1725 N St. N.W.
Washington, DC 20036
202/223-4383, fax 202/223-4391

MOLDOVA
Embassy of Moldova
2101 S St. N.W.
Washington, DC 20008
202/667-1130, fax 202/667-1204

MONGOLIA
Embassy of Mongolia
2833 M St. N.W.
Washington, DC 20007
202/333-7117, fax 202/298-9227

MOROCCO
Embassy of Morocco
1601 21st St. N.W.
Washington, DC 20009
202/462-7979, fax 202/265-0161

MOZAMBIQUE
Embassy of Mozambique
1990 M St. N.W. #570
Washington, DC 20036
202/293-7146, fax 202/835-0245

MYANMAR (Burma)
Embassy of the Union of Burma
2300 S St. N.W.
Washington, DC 20008
202/332-9044, fax 202/332-9046

NAMIBIA
Embassy of Namibia
1603 New Hampshire Ave. N.W.
Washington, DC 20009
202/986-0540, fax 202/986-0443

NEPAL
Embassy of Nepal
2131 Leroy Pl. N.W.
Washington, DC 20008
202/667-4550, fax 202/667-5534

NETHERLANDS
Embassy of the Netherlands
4200 Linnean Ave. N.W.
Washington, DC 20008
202/244-5300, fax 202/362-3430

NEW ZEALAND
Embassy of New Zealand
37 Observatory Circle N.W.
Washington, DC 20008
202/328-4800

NICARAGUA
Embassy of Nicaragua
1627 New Hampshire Ave. N.W.
Washington, DC 20009
202/939-6570

NIGER
Embassy of Niger
2204 R St. N.W.
Washington, DC 20008
202/483-4224

NIGERIA
Embassy of Nigeria
1333 16th St. N.W.
Washington, DC 20036
202/986-8400

NORWAY
Embassy of Norway
2720 34th St. N.W.
Washington, DC 20008
202/333-6000, fax 202/337-0870

OMAN
Embassy of Oman
2535 Belmont Rd. N.W.
Washington, DC 20008
202/387-1980, fax 202/745-4933

PAKISTAN
Embassy of Pakistan
2315 Massachusetts Ave. N.W.
Washington, DC 20008
202/939-6205, fax 202/387-0484

PALAU
Embassy of Palau
1150 18th St. N.W. #750
Washington, DC 20008
202/452-6814, fax 202/452-6281

PANAMA
Embassy of Panama
2862 McGill Terrace N.W.
Washington, DC 20008
202/483-1407

PAPAU NEW GUINEA
Embassy of Papau New Guinea
1615 New Hampshire Ave. N.W.
Third Floor
Washington, DC 20009
202/745-3680, fax 202/745-3679

PARAGUAY
Embassy of Paraguay
2400 Massachusetts Ave. N.W.
Washington, DC 20008
202/483-6960, fax 202/234-4508

PERU
Embassy of Peru
1700 Massachusetts Ave. N.W.
Washington, DC 20036
202/833-9860, fax 202/659-8124

PHILIPPINES
Embassy of the Philippines
1600 Massachusetts Ave. N.W.
Washington, DC 20036
202/467-9300, fax 202/328-7614

POLAND
Embassy of Poland
3640 16th St. N.W.
Washington, DC 20009
202/234-3800, fax 202/328-6271

PORTUGAL
Embassy of Portugal
2125 Kalorama Rd. N.W.
Washington, DC 20008
202/328-8610, fax 202/462-3726

QATAR
Embassy of the State of Qatar
4200 Wisconsin Ave. N.W.
Washington, DC 20016
202/274-1600

ROMANIA

Embassy of Romania
1607 23rd St. N.W.
Washington, DC 20008
202/332-4846, fax 202/232-4748

RUSSIA

Embassy of the
Russian Federation
2650 Wisconsin Ave. N.W.
Washington, DC 20007
202/298-5700, fax 202/298-5735

RWANDA

Embassy of the
Republic of Rwanda
1714 New Hampshire Ave. N.W.
Washington, DC 20009
202/232-2882, fax 202/232-4544

SAINT KITTS AND NEVIS

Embassy of Saint Kitts and Nevis
3216 New Mexico Ave. N.W.
Washington, DC 20016
202/686-2636, fax 202/686-5740

SAINT LUCIA

Embassy of Saint Lucia
3216 New Mexico Ave. N.W.
Washington, DC 20016
202/364-6792, fax 202/364-6728

SAINT VINCENT AND THE GRENADINES

Embassy of Saint Vincent
and the Grenadines
3216 New Mexico Ave. N.W.
Washington, DC 20016
202/364-6730, fax 202/364-6736

SAMOA

Embassy of the Independent
State of Samoa, UN Mission
800 Second Ave., Suite 400D
New York, NY 10017
212/599-6196, fax 212/599-0797

SAO TOME AND PRINCIPE

122 E. 42nd St. #1604
New York, NY 10168
212/697-4211, fax 212/687-8389

SAUDI ARABIA

Embassy of Saudi Arabia
601 New Hampshire Ave. N.W.
Washington, DC 20037
202/342-3800

SENEGAL

Embassy of the
Republic of Senegal
2112 Wyoming Ave., N.W.
Washington, DC 20008
202/234-0540

SEYCHELLES

Embassy of the Republic of
Seychelles, UN Mission
800 Second Ave., Suite 400C
New York, NY 10017
212/972-1785, fax 212/972-1786

SIERRA LEONE
Embassy of Sierra Leone
1701 19th St. N.W.
Washington, DC 20009
202/939-9261
fax 202/483-1793

SINGAPORE
Embassy of the
Republic of Singapore
3501 International Place N.W.
Washington, DC 20008
202/537-3100, fax 202/537-0876

SLOVAKIA
Embassy of the Slovak Republic
2201 Wisconsin Ave. N.W.
Suite 250
Washington, DC 20007
202/965-5161, fax 202/965-5166

SLOVENIA
Embassy of the
Republic of Slovenia
1525 New Hampshire Ave. N.W.
Washington, DC 20036
202/667-5363, fax 202/6674563

SOLOMON ISLANDS
Embassy of the Solomon Islands
UN Mission, 800 Second Ave.
Suite 400L
New York, NY 10017
212/599-6192/93
fax 212/661-8925

SOUTH AFRICA
Embassy of the Republic of
South Africa
3051 Massachusetts Ave. N.W.
Washington, DC 20008
202/232-4400, fax 202/265-1607

SPAIN
Embassy of Spain
2375 Pennsylvania Ave. N.W.
Washington, DC 20037
202/452-0100, fax 202/833-5670

SRI LANKA
Embassy of the Democratic
Socialist Republic of Sri Lanka
2148 Wyoming Ave. N.W.
Washington, DC 20008
202/483-4025, fax 202/232-7181

SUDAN
Embassy of the
Republic of the Sudan
2210 Massachusetts Ave. N.W.
Washington, DC 20008
202/338-8565, fax 202/667-2406

SURINAME
Embassy of the
Republic of Suriname
4301 Connecticut Ave. N.W.
Suite 460
Washington, DC 20008
202/244-7488, fax 202/244-5878

SWAZILAND
Embassy of the
Kingdom of Swaziland
3400 International Dr. N.W.
Washington, DC 20008
202/362-6683, fax 202/244-8059

SWEDEN
Embassy of Sweden
1501 M St. N.W.
Washington, DC 20005
202/467-2600, fax 202/467-2699

SWITZERLAND
Embassy of Switzerland
2900 Cathedral Ave. N.W.
Washington, DC 20008
202/745-7900, fax 202/387-2564

SYRIA
Embassy of the
Syrian Arab Republic
2215 Wyoming Ave. N.W.
Washington, DC 20008
202/232-6313, fax 202/234-9548

TANZANIA
Embassy of the United Republic
of Tanzania
2139 R St. N.W.
Washington, DC 20008
202/939-6125, fax 202/797-7408

THAILAND
Royal Thai Embassy
1024 Wisconsin Ave. N.W.
Washington, DC 20007
202/944-3600, fax 202/944-3611

TOGO
Embassy of the Republic of Togo
2208 Massachusetts Ave. N.W.
Washington, DC 20008
202/234-4212, fax 202/232-3190

TRINIDAD AND TOBAGO
Embassy of the Republic of
Trinidad and Tobago
1708 Massachusetts Ave. N.W.
Washington, DC 20036
202/467-6490, fax 202/785-3130

TUNISIA
Embassy of Tunisia
1515 Massachusetts Ave. N.W.
Washington, DC 20005
202/862-1850

TURKEY
Embassy of the
Republic of Turkey
1714 Massachusetts Ave. N.W.
Washington, DC 20036
202/659-8200, fax 202/659-0744

TURKMENISTAN
Embassy of Turkmenistan
2207 Massachusetts Ave. N.W.
Washington, DC 20008
202/588-1500, fax 202/588-0697

UGANDA
Embassy of the
Republic of Uganda
5911 16th St. N.W.
Washington, DC 20011
202/726-7100, fax 202/726-1727

UKRAINE

Embassy of Ukraine
3350 M St. N.W.
Washington, DC 20007
202/333-0606, fax 202/333-0817

UNITED ARAB EMIRATES

Embassy of the
United Arab Emirates
1255 22nd St. N.W., Suite 700
Washington, DC 20037
202/955-7999

UNITED KINGDOM OF GREAT BRITAIN AND NORTHERN IRELAND

British Embassy
3100 Massachusetts Ave. N.W.
Washington, DC 20008
202/588-6500, fax 202/588-7870

URUGUAY

Embassy of Uruguay
2715 M St. N.W.
Washington, DC 20007
202/331-1313, fax 202/331-8142

UZBEKISTAN

Embassy of the
Republic of Uzbekistan
1746 Massachusetts Ave. N.W.
Washington, DC 20036
202/887 5300, fax 202/293-6804

VENEZUELA

Embassy of the
Republic of Venezuela
1099 30th St., N.W.
Washington, DC 20007
202/342-2214, fax 202/342-6820

VIETNAM

Embassy of Vietnam
1233 20th St., N.W. Suite 400
Washington, DC 20036
202/861-0737, fax 202/861-0917

YEMEN

Embassy of the
Republic of Yemen
2600 Virginia Ave. N.W., Suite 705
Washington, DC 20037
202/965-4760, fax 202/337-2017

YUGOSLAVIA

Embassy of Yugoslavia
2410 California St. N.W.
Washington, DC 20008
202/462-6566

ZAIRE (See Congo)

ZAMBIA

Embassy of Zambia
2419 Massachusetts Ave. N.W.
Washington, DC 20008
202/265-9717, fax 202/332-0826

ZIMBABWE

Embassy of Zimbabwe
1608 New Hampshire Ave. N.W.
Washington, DC 20009
202/332-7100, fax 202/483-9326

Index

Rutledge Photographics

About the Author

After earning a master's degree in comparative literature from the University of Washington, Nancy Mueller went on to teach English as a second language, first in the United States, then in Cairo, Egypt. She later worked as a consultant on cross-cultural communications in Europe and as director of the EF Language Schools in Olympia, Washington. Her travels have taken her to Brazil, Hong Kong, and China.

Nancy currently runs International Adaptations, which offers workshops on business communication skills, cross-cultural communications, and international protocol. She and her husband, John, live in Seattle. They recently adopted a baby girl from China.